INTO THE WILDERNESS

Photographed by Lowell Georgia
Illustrated by H. Tom Hall

Prepared by the Special Publications Division
National Geographic Society, Washington, D. C.

Foreword

Above the Arctic Circle at midnight, when the August sun gently kisses the horizon, the mighty Mackenzie River reflects a spectrum of brilliance. Here, as Alexander Mackenzie left it in 1789, this silent river still glides rhythmically to the Arctic Ocean—still, after almost two centuries, untamed and unmarred. How could this magnificent spectacle ever have been one man's river of disappointment?

This exquisite moment, accented by the stillness of air and the vastness of river and sky, held me hypnotized in the footsteps of Canada's great explorer.

What a glorious beginning to a nine-month adventure that would take me across five provinces of Canada and twenty-two of the United States! I would follow the trails of explorers whose varied lives led them to unknown horizons, along trails now pathways of history. My challenge was to identify settings of their work, capture scenes they saw at the appropriate seasons in similar weather, record the wilderness they knew where it still survives.

Along these trails, I know I shared some of their impres-

INTO THE WILDERNESS
RON FISHER, JOHN HESS, THOMAS O'NEILL,
  CYNTHIA RUSS RAMSAY, MICHAEL W. ROBBINS,
  RICHARD T. SALE, EDWARD O. WELLES, JR.,
  Contributing Authors

Published by
THE NATIONAL GEOGRAPHIC SOCIETY
GILBERT M. GROSVENOR, *President*
MELVIN M. PAYNE, *Chairman of the Board*
OWEN R. ANDERSON, *Executive Vice President*
ROBERT L. BREEDEN, *Vice President,*
  Publications and Educational Media

Prepared by
THE SPECIAL PUBLICATIONS DIVISION
DONALD J. CRUMP, *Editor*
PHILIP B. SILCOTT, *Associate Editor*
MARY ANN HARRELL, *Managing Editor*
JENNIFER URQUHART, BONNIE S. LAWRENCE,
  Research
BARBARA PAYNE, *Research Assistant*

Illustrations and Design
JOHN AGNONE, *Picture Editor*
URSULA PERRIN VOSSELER, *Art Director*
RON FISHER, DANIEL E. HUTNER, JANE R.
  MCCAULEY, H. ROBERT MORRISON, CYNTHIA
  RUSS RAMSAY, MICHAEL W. ROBBINS,
  EDWARD O. WELLES, JR., *Picture Legends*
JOHN D. GARST, JR., CHARLES W. BERRY,
  MARGARET DEANE GRAY, ALFRED L. ZEBARTH,
  Map Research, Design, and Production

sions. I felt a tinge of panic at being lost . . . the madness of no escape from black flies and mosquitoes in an Arctic summer . . . the shortness of breath and the paradoxical burning sensation of nose and cheeks in minus 40° cold.

I knew the weight of loneliness as I stood beneath a heavy, slate-gray sky on the barren coast of Hudson Bay, where surveyor David Thompson first landed as a boy of 14.

Moving through the humid low country of Georgia, with William Bartram's verbal and artistic portraits at hand, I could touch the complexity of life in this floral web.

Other adventurers of destiny — Lewis and Clark, John Charles Frémont, Kit Carson, the friars Escalante and Domínguez, Daniel Boone and the grizzled mountain men — took me along to share their vistas and byways of solitude.

Take this book to a quiet place . . . stand beside the trails now made famous by history. As you read, pause now and then to listen carefully for the sounds of their footsteps — you are no longer separated in time.

Lowell Georgia

Production and Printing
ROBERT W. MESSER, *Production Manager*
GEORGE V. WHITE, *Assistant Production Manager*
RAJA D. MURSHED, JUNE L. GRAHAM, CHRISTINE A. ROBERTS, DAVID V. SHOWERS, *Production Assistants*
DEBRA A. ANTONINI, BARBARA BRICKS, JANE H. BUXTON, ROSAMUND GARNER, SUZANNE J. JACOBSON, AMY E. METCALFE, CLEO PETROFF, KATHERYN M. SLOCUM, SUZANNE VENINO, *Staff Assistants*
MARTHA K. HIGHTOWER, *Index*

Above: Sutter Buttes in the Sacramento Valley, a rich prize in the American takeover of California. Preceding pages: midnight sun over the Mackenzie River. Page 1: American bison — watercolor by naturalist Mark Catesby, c. 1724. Endpapers: modern-day mountain men Lance Grabowski and Jon Judd, in Utah's Wasatch country. Hardcover illustration: coastal forest in California, on the route taken by explorer Jedediah Smith in 1828.

Library of Congress CIP Data: page 207

Contents

Baneberry in August, British Columbia

Weathered sandstone creates a realm of desolate splendor in northern

1 Domínguez and Escalante

Arizona, along the route of the Domínguez-Escalante expedition in 1776.

in the Southwest

By CYNTHIA RUSS RAMSAY

In the bright glare of morning, ten riders angle north across the sunbaked land, leaving behind the narrow, winding streets of the city of the Holy Faith—Santa Fe. The road, a faint scar on threadbare soil, clambers up a ridge away from the capital of the Spanish empire's remote province of New Mexico.

The horses and mules kick up plumes of red dust that cloud a last glimpse of the capital, a town 166 years old in the summer of 1776 but still little more than a huddle of adobe houses and churches for some 1,300 Spaniards, mestizos, and Indians.

Ahead, great vistas sweep across the land's vast expanse. Juniper-studded hills roll toward mesas with sheer walls like medieval ramparts for a kingdom of giants. In the far distance, jagged peaks outline the fierce blue sky.

A landscape of sky and rock that engulfs me in silence.

My eyes are probing the distances scanned by the Hispanic travelers 201 years ago, as they set out on what historian Herbert E. Bolton calls "one of the great exploring expeditions of North American history, made without noise of arms and without giving offense to the natives through whose country they traveled."

Two Franciscans, Fray Francisco Atanasio Domínguez, about 36, and his younger partner Fray Silvestre Vélez de Escalante, led their party nearly 2,000 miles in a wide, wavering circle from Santa Fe. Departing on July 29, 1776, the padres headed northwest through the spruce and aspen forests of Colorado, across northern Utah, and then south down the melancholy empty spaces of the Great Basin. Finally in October, after a two-day snowstorm, they urged their men toward home. The weary band turned east across northern Arizona, a spectacular land slashed by canyons, soaring buttes, and sky-high ridges.

I traveled to many of the same places. A diary of the expedition, meticulously kept by the fathers, gives such detailed descriptions of terrain and such accurate estimates of distance that students of the journey have been able to plot virtually the exact route. Distances were calculated in *leguas,* leagues—a measure based on how far a horseman can go in an hour at a walk over level ground. With few exceptions the padres did not cover more than 9 leagues, or about 24 miles, a day.

For me the landscape was not something to conquer or to survive—it was something to admire and enjoy. I said as much to Bill Daley as we reined in our horses and watched the glow of sunset stain Arizona's Hurricane Cliffs before the fading light transformed them into shadows against the mauve sky.

It had been a glorious day. Sunlight turned the grama grass into sprays of gold against the ocher earth and gray-green sagebrush; a lone eagle dipped and soared above a sandstone bluff; and the hoofbeats of our horses added a quiet, steady rhythm to the stillness of the desert. We had jounced along at an easy pace, covering the 15 miles of the day's itinerary in exuberant spirits.

But Bill, my guide along the Arizona strip, had seen such days from another perspective: "Fifteen or twenty miles a day may seem like the easiest thing to do unless you're taking care of your horse, saddling it, breaking camp, riding all day, and you know you're going to have to do it over again, day after day."

Bill, an ardent outdoorsman, had ridden the entire Domínguez-Escalante trail for four months in 1976. To commemorate the journey of the padres for the American Bicentennial, he had led four women and eight men in an expedition on horseback that followed as closely as possible the original route.

"We had a different set of challenges," he said as we rode toward the campsite on the crest of a mesa. In the dimmed light, Bill with his glittering eyes, long glossy mustache, and easy slouch in the saddle might have been one of the soldiers in the army of a conquistador. Only his parka looked out of place.

Thoughts of steaming coffee urged us to hurry. Then we met, head-on, one of those challenges Bill had mentioned.

On the morning of departure, July 29, 1776, ten explorers ride out of Santa Fe. Led by two Franciscan priests, Father Francisco Atanasio Domínguez and Father Silvestre Vélez de

Fences. Miles and miles of fence as far as we could see. I slid off my horse and followed the barbed wire on and on, unmindful of the glitter of a million stars, intent only on finding the gate.

"These days even when you leave the pavement, there are fences, rules, and restrictions. Even where the land is as wild as it ever was, now it's whittled down to a patch. It is not the wilderness the padres knew," Bill grumbled in the darkness.

The early Spanish explorers were lured into the American West by legends of gold. Later, to the north, because beaver hats were the rage in Europe, traders and trappers followed rivers and streams into the wilderness to seek fortunes in fur. The wilderness also promised land for the hungry and a second chance

Escalante, they sought an overland route from the New Mexico colony to Monterey in California. The friars, who kept a detailed record of their travels, hoped to carry the Christian faith to Indians along the way.

Utah:
The Destination
Worthy of a Dream

September snow dusts summits of the Wasatch Range near Utah's Spanish Fork Canyon, not far from the padres' route. Below the knife-edge ridges, coneflowers blossom in a lush meadow. Through a landscape of "perilous defiles" and thickets dense with chokecherry and scrub oak, a guide called Silvestre led the explorers down to a broad valley. There his tribe fished and hunted small game on the shores of Utah Lake. These gentle-mannered people seemed eager to accept Christianity. For the padres, who by late September had covered almost a thousand miles of rugged terrain among hostile tribes, this valley "with good land for crops. . . . [and] abundant pastures," with sufficient water and peaceful Indians, seemed the ideal place for a mission.

The Route:
An Unyielding Land

In a land of little moisture and meager soil, sagebrush spreads across the Great Basin in western Utah. Here, as the explorers pushed south from Utah Lake, finding water fit to drink became a daily ordeal. Dwindling food supplies added to their hardship in a region too arid to support abundant game. At left, a cottontail ventures onto the sunbaked flats. For Indians who roamed this inhospitable land—the Pavant or "bearded" Utes—rabbits provided not only food but also skins cut into strips and woven for clothing. A formidable predator of small mammals and birds, a sleek bobcat emerges warily from a rock shelter.

for the unsuccessful or those just one step ahead of the law, and pathfinders were paid to lead the way for wagon trains west. Then, to the last harsh and lonely strongholds of the wild went the pick-and-shovel prospectors in quest of the big bonanza. And always the wilderness beckoned to the restless spirits infected with the fever to see what was on the other side.

But neither dreams nor discontent impelled the Domínguez-Escalante mission through the uncharted wilderness. Instead it was a political motive—the urgent need for a route by which Spain could supply and settle the feeble and impoverished fledgling colony of Alta California.

While insurgents were fomenting revolution in the 13 colonies on the east coast of North America, the Spanish viceroy in Mexico City was concerned with the survival of his new province. In 1773 a total population of 11 friars and 60 soldiers held the Upper California colony—no match for the Russian fur traders exploiting Alaska and the British lurking in Pacific waters. Ships were too small and ocean winds too unfavorable to send people

and goods by sea from Mexico. An overland route connecting Santa Fe with Monterey seemed to offer a solution.

Early in 1776 Father Domínguez was sent from his native Mexico City to inspect the missions of New Mexico and seek such a route. He and Father Escalante, a Spanish-born missionary in the Zuni pueblo, organized their expedition accordingly.

For his expedition 200 years later, Bill Daley chose from 100 applicants who had answered an ad in a horseman's journal. He picked those with tenacity and determination: "Aside from skills or physical strength, we needed just the will to stick it out."

The padres had other criteria. Among the group they assembled was a versatile gentleman, Don Bernardo Miera y Pacheco, man at arms and engineer, artist, and cartographer. Miera checked the expedition's progress with his compass and his quadrant, an instrument used to determine latitude. The map he later drew remained a standard reference for the vast reaches of the Great Basin until the mid-19th century.

Another recruit, the interpreter Andrés Muñiz, was a veteran of earlier sorties into the precipitous country of the Ute Indians in what is now southwestern Colorado.

Since the Juan María de Rivera expedition in 1765, prospectors and traders had threaded the Indian trails well beyond New Mexico's beleaguered outposts of Taos and Abiquiu, into Colorado and perhaps as far as Utah. Those men were searching for silver and bartering knives, cloth, beads, and horses for deerskins and dried meat. According to passing references in Spanish documents, the Utes traded children into slavery. These were probably captives from other tribes.

The Spanish often freed these youngsters when they grew up, and sometimes ransomed other captives from the Plains tribes. They and their descendants became a caste of Indians called *genízaros,* with a Christian upbringing and Spanish ways.

Muñiz, his brother, three other genízaros, and two other Spaniards made up the rest of the party, all undoubtedly sharing the hardy spirit that seems to come to people who live on the edge of danger. For the entire New Mexico colony was still a frontier zone of small Spanish settlements and Indian pueblos, with a Spanish pastor or two, scattered across unoccupied country.

"In the east," explained Fray Angelico Chavez, "settlers by their sheer numbers just gradually pushed the Indians out, but here the Comanches, Navajos, Apaches, and Utes came down from the mountains and across the plains in countless bloody raids. The Indians, you see, often preferred to steal their horses rather than trade for them. . . ."

I had arranged to meet Father Chavez in Santa Fe. It was his recent translation of the expedition's journal that I had been reading. And no one could give me better insight into the kind of men the padres were than this poet, writer, and historian, a descendant of the earliest Spanish settlers and formerly, for 41 years, a member of the Franciscan order. This wisp of a man knows the life that Domínguez and Escalante had entered by taking the Franciscan vows of poverty, chastity, and obedience.

"From time to time the journal gives us a glimpse into the character of the two friars," Father Chavez commented with his wry smile. "Some phrases, especially the occasional sarcasm, sound like Domínguez, the stern perfectionist who wrote such a scathing report on the missions of New Mexico. Escalante was the more optimistic and enthusiastic man—obviously a much sweeter personality."

I told Father Chavez I was trying to imagine how Domínguez and Escalante felt as they urged their horses beyond the last landmark—and contemplated distances that had no bounds, with Monterey near latitude 36° North, somewhere to the west.

In his opinion, the padres were men without fear. Theirs was a divine task. "They believed they would either establish new missions, or they would find martyrdom. Either way their names would go down in the annals of the order. They may have set forth to serve the king and the empire, but they were first and foremost devout priests and fervent missionaries. They were looking for converts and likely places for settlements.

"Look in the journal. For the most part Escalante reserved his enthusiasm for scenery that had pasture for livestock, land suitable for farming, and timber on the hills for firewood."

I learned from Father Chavez to what extent Domínguez and Escalante were heirs to a long tradition of pioneer clerics riding a trail into the unknown. Friars in coarse robes had accompanied the dashing Hernando de Soto in 1539 on his relentless three-year hunt for treasure across the southeast and in the lower Mississippi Valley. It was a Franciscan who led Vásquez de Coronado in the futile quest for the golden cities of Cibola in 1540. After Spain abandoned the region, disappointed by Coronado's failure, it was missionary zeal that rekindled interest in the American southwest.

Even in the 18th century, when Spanish fervor for exploration had subsided, the padres persevered. There was Father Francisco Garcés. With his pack mules and Indian guides he walked his way across the parched wastes of the southwest. In 1776 he tried a southerly route from California toward New Mexico. But his route was so short of water and pasturage and the Indians so hostile that his efforts only raised more hopes for the Domínguez-Escalante venture via the northwest.

As Father Chavez talked we ambled through the old plaza of Santa Fe. Along the arcade outside the Governor's Palace, Indian women wrapped to the eyes in striped blankets sat beside their wares of silver and turquoise jewelry—bold and heavy Navajo designs, delicate flowerlike mosaics in the Zuni style. We turned down a street and stopped at a little cubicle of a shop fragrant with spices and herbs. On the wall hung bright red chili peppers strung together in long banners called *ristras*.

"I bet the padres took along chilies," said Father Chavez, "but we can only guess, because like most people who keep journals Escalante did not record the commonplace. We know they took chocolate, which they used instead of coffee. We assume they also packed salt, jerked beef, dried chick peas and lentils, corn and wheat for tortillas, and little cones of brown sugar."

Against the rain the men wore tightly woven wool serapes that they used on the hard ground when they slept.

No tents or down sleeping bags, no rain ponchos or the freeze-dried precooked meals that ease my pampered sorties into the wilderness. Not even matches. Instead they struck a steel blade against flint and caught the sparks on a cotton wick.

The padres were a few days out of Abiquiu, the last town they would see for nearly four months, when the guides failed

To end dissension and settle the course of the party, the men "inquire . . . the will of God by means of casting lots." The friars, anxious to prepare for a mission among the

Utes, wanted to abandon the search for a way west. An early snowstorm on October 5 made this seem more prudent. But others, anticipating riches and glory from the discovery of a trade route, threatened to rebel. All, however, accepted the verdict of the lots—and they headed southeast toward home.

them. Escalante, clearly irritated, wrote of struggling "through canyons, over hills, and through very difficult brush. The guides lost the trail and even seemed to have forgotten the very slight knowledge which they had appeared to have of this country."

That annoyance was nothing compared to the frustration of trying to follow the Dolores River. The river spills out of a jumble of mountains called the San Juans and twists through the flanks of the Uncompahgre Plateau, carving a "tall and craggy" canyon in blood-red sandstone. Scores of streams tumbling down to the Dolores honeycomb the plateau with side-canyons that go nowhere and slice it into an impassable network of mesas.

For three days the men traced the Dolores through a gorge that seemed to wander aimlessly—and endlessly. They could not decide whether to keep trying or to take the trail to the east, where they might find a guide among the Sabuagana Utes.

So the padres resorted to a device common at the time.

A Spanish Domain

Sierras and streams web a map by the expedition's cartographer, Don Bernardo Miera y Pacheco, with impressive accuracy for the region he saw. But he erred when he extended Utah Lake ("Laguna de los Timpanogos") to include Great Salt Lake. He drew the mythical Tizon River flowing westward, and showed the Green River ("Río de

Spanning four states, the Domínguez-Escalante trail meanders nearly 2,000 miles across deserts, mesas, mountains, and canyons. The party followed a route used by local traders toward Colorado, and traveled with Ute guides as far as southern Utah. Then, with only vague directions from Paiutes, they had to discover their own way across the Colorado River. When they reached the Hopi pueblos in northeastern Arizona, they knew the way home.

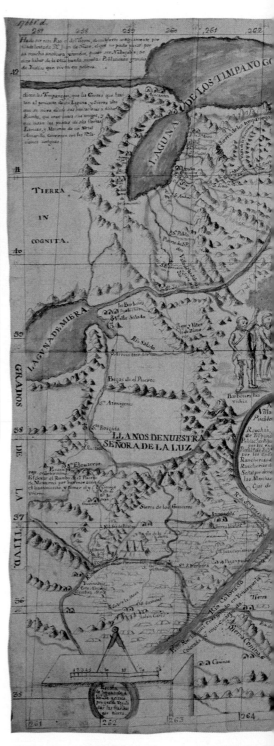

San Buenaventura") crossing the Rockies into a Laguna de Miera. Thus he perpetuated the notion that a waterway linked the interior of the continent with the Pacific. Miera enriched this map with pictures of bearded Utes and of the Pope, riding in a golden car of state drawn by lions that symbolize the power of Spain.

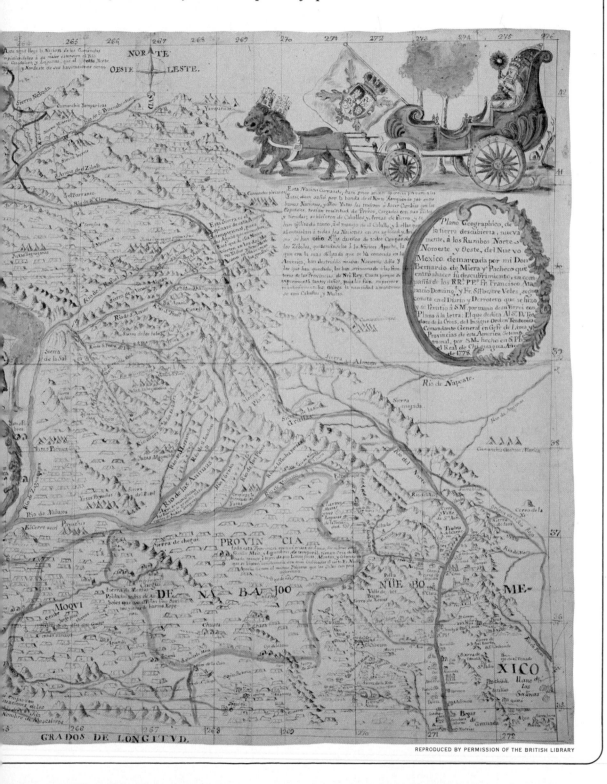

Swift and deep, the Colorado knifes into Marble Canyon. Upstream, the padres spent 13 harrowing days seeking a usable crossing. Downstream, the river enters the gorge of the Grand Canyon, of which Indians had warned the party. On the rim, boulders eroded by storm winds and rain mark a "very troublesome" landscape.

Escalante wrote: "we put our trust in God and our will in that of His most holy Majesty; then, after begging the intercession of our thrice-holy patron saints that God might direct us . . . to His most holy service, we cast lots. . . ."

They drew the direction of the Sabuaganas, and on August 20 began a long detour to the east, climbing out of the Dolores Canyon to a ridge so rugged that many of the animals "left their tracks on the stones with the blood from their feet."

Three days later they encountered the first Indian they had seen for weeks, a Ute who agreed to lead them to the Sabuagana camp in return for two big knives and 16 strings of white glass beads. He may have told them of a lake to the northwest where Utes called Lagunas, or Timpanogotzis, were living.

In any case, the padres found some of these Lagunas in the Sabuagana camp. The visitors had come more than 300 miles to trade for horses, and one, called Silvestre by the padres, promised to guide them to his homeland.

"The country was full of trails—trails that followed game, that led to water, the best grass, or the easiest way across the mountains," said Calvin Hackler, a tall angular Westerner. He owns a guest ranch just outside Collbran, Colorado, a town where grizzled old-timers in Stetsons tell tales of the days when gunslingers could split a card edgewise and hunters could track a grasshopper against the wind.

Cal often leads pack trips along old Ute trails, and he took me up the mile-high flanks of the Grand Mesa—to the lush meadows, thick stands of spruce and aspen, and three hundred lakes on the summit. The padres crossed it on their way to the Sabuagana encampment of thirty skin tents.

There, at the edge of the Grand Mesa, Father Domínguez with crucifix in hand preached to the Indians through Muñiz, the interpreter. In turn they tried to discourage the padres from entering the perilous Comanche country ahead.

Escalante suspected the Muñiz brothers of "secretly prompting" the Sabuaganas, perhaps out of fear. The same two provoked him further by violating orders against trading with the Indians. The entry for September 1 is unmistakably angry and sarcastic: "Andrés . . . with his brother Lucrecio . . . most greedily sought weapons [bows and arrows] from the infidels. . . . to our own sorrow, they betrayed their meager faith or lack of it, and how very unfit they were for ventures of this kind."

When the Sabuaganas were breaking camp, the padres departed "with utmost pleasure." With them went Silvestre, some fresh horses, and a Laguna boy they called Joaquín.

As the expedition crossed the highlands into Utah, summer ripened into autumn, and the aspens spangled the forests with gold. The bright leaves fluttering and trembling among the stands of dark spruce shimmered like doubloons spilling from a chest in the dead of night.

"Silvestre knew the way just as surely as if he were following a road map," said Monsignor Jerome Stoffel as we drove west across the Uinta Basin to the Wasatch Range. "Without hesitating he took the padres across the Green River at a little-used ford—a well-known one was about sixty miles south."

Monsignor Stoffel had taken a day from his duties to show me the route of the padres and share with me his enthusiasm for the dogged men in that lonely little procession across the west. He knew all the places Escalante described in the Uinta Basin— the juniper-covered plateaus, the plunging cliffs, the ravines choked with dense scrub oak and brush. He pointed out where Silvestre skirted the roughest terrain when he could. "But Silvestre had to steer clear of the easiest routes along exposed ridges to avoid being seen by the hostile Comanches."

On September 23, the padres descended to the wide Utah Valley, where they found the Laguna Indians "very simple, docile, gentle, and affectionate" and eager to become Christians. For nearly a thousand miles, Escalante had been careful to note any "good land for crops." Here in the Utah Valley, where apple and cherry trees bloom today, was the site the padres were looking for.

The diary lists the splendid advantages of the valley, and details of life for a Ute tribe that had not yet become dependent on the horse. The Indians lived on the lake's abundant fish . . . they gathered wild seeds for gruel . . . they hunted jackrabbits and birds. . . . "Their dwellings are some sheds or little wattle huts. . . . They are very poor as regards dress."

The padres promised to return soon "when all, big and small, would be baptized."

Then the padres turned south, hoping to find other guides because the Lagunas knew nothing of the lands to the west.

The next segment of the Domínguez-Escalante trail led me into the barren desolation of the Sevier Desert. I set out from Provo, Utah, with two of the nicest professors I've ever met—Ted Warner and Tom Alexander teach history at Brigham Young University. The lesson I learned was unexpected.

We followed a tracery of jeep trails through a sparse stubble of sagebrush. To our left, the Wasatch Range formed a mighty wall stretching south. Mile after mile of unending bleak sameness rolled by, relieved only by the animated conversation of my companions. "I think once the padres saw the Utah Valley they were ready to postpone the Monterey business—they just wanted to get to Santa Fe and arrange a mission to the Lagunas."

Our car interrupted Ted by wedging itself in deep sand.

Tom and Ted, struggling to dig it out, thought I might summon help from a waterfowl refuge, nine miles west. I started walking. No landmarks; only sagebrush shivering in the wind.

This was closer to the way the padres saw the land, I thought, but they had no idea of what they would encounter next. And I

Through this notch called Gunsight Pass, the explorers could have picked their way down a narrow slickrock trail from the canyon rim toward the bank of the Colorado—the best route possible, say authorities on the local terrain. But the padres missed this shortcut. Suffering from cold and drenched by rainstorms, they struggled on.

Pages 26-27: In a tortuous descent to Padre Creek, the weary men hack shallow footholds for their horses along ten feet of a tricky sandstone slope—last hazard before the creekbed and the riverbank.

knew that if I missed the refuge I might never find anyone. . . . I hurried back to rejoin Ted and Tom, and we walked toward the refuge lights as dusk fell. "This is one way to correct your awareness of distance," said Tom. "We're too accustomed to seeing things while doing 55 down the highway."

Each step took the padres farther south and into the sullen reaches of the Escalante Desert. Each day began and ended with a search for an arroyo with pasture, without brackish water. Along the way the expedition met small groups of Indians—Paiute bands who could tell nothing of the land to the west.

On the evening of October 5, snow began to fall, continuing all the next day. The expedition was approaching the supposed latitude of Monterey; but after the blizzard, when the padres looked to the west, they saw that the succession of peaks on the horizon lay under snow. Winter had arrived early, and the padres feared snow would soon seal off the mountain passes. It had already turned the alkaline flats of the desert into a quagmire where "many pack animals and saddle horses . . . either fell down or mired in the mud."

In camp on the night of October 8, Domínguez and Escalante decided to go straight to Santa Fe. They were anxious to return, as they had promised, to the Lagunas. Delay "might be very harmful to the souls who . . . desired their eternal salvation through holy baptism."

Miera, who saw the glory of discovering a trade route slipping away, resented the decision and goaded the others into insubordination. Escalante wrote: "Everything was now very onerous to them and everything insufferably difficult."

So the padres "decided to inquire anew the will of God by means of casting lots."

There was no more dissension. The expedition would return to Santa Fe through the land of the Cosninas (Havasupai Indians) who lived in the great gorge of the Río Colorado somewhere to the southeast.

As the group moved south toward what is now Arizona, they came upon Paiute women gathering grass seeds. "These Indian women were so poorly dressed that they wore only some pieces of buckskin hanging from their waists, which hardly covered what can not be looked at without peril."

"Poor Paiutes," I had said to Bill Daley. "They really lived at the most primitive level."

Waters of Lake Powell—impounded by Glen Canyon Dam 16 miles downstream—drown the site of the Crossing of the Fathers, where the party forded the river on November 7, "praising God our Lord" and firing muskets in "great joy." Beyond Dominguez Butte (foreground) the expedition found a campsite with "good pasturage and plenty of rainwater." From this spot they headed south and then east, to the villages of the Hopi.

Strongholds of Faith Among the Hopi

In the midsummer rite of the Home Dance, photographed in 1901, a priest in white sprinkles sacred cornmeal on a procession of dancers—a form of prayer for rain. In Hopi belief, these cult dancers become the incarnations of spirits called kachinas, *whose masks they wear. On their way, Domínguez and Escalante tried to win converts among the Hopi, but failed as have countless others. Now as in centuries past, the deeply religious Hopi still worship the deities of their ancestors.*

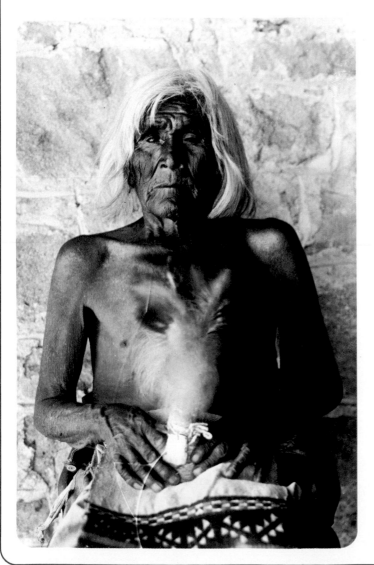

Holding a sacred tiponi— *a badge of religious office made from an ear of corn, string, and feathers—the noted dignitary Chasra sits for a portrait in 1901. Turn-of-the-century photographer Adam Clark Vroman recorded ritual life. Today the Hopi guard their privacy more closely and have banned cameras from their ceremonies.*

Stone houses of Walpi overlook the desert, little changed in 1901 from the village where the padres found shelter for the night of November 18, 1776. The Indians welcomed them "very joyfully," professing friendship, asking Spanish protection against enemy attacks, but firmly refusing to abandon traditions of "foolish impiety."

Bill shot right back: "Some people would say the Paiutes were very skilled to be able to eke a living out of this country."

Sheer beauty, not rich soil or grasslands full of game, characterizes the land in the southeast corner of Utah and the Arizona strip. And what for me was a journey into an Eden of stone in the canyonlands of the Colorado was a 13-day ordeal for the Domínguez-Escalante expedition. Without guides to help them, they had to grope for a way across the river.

When the padres arrived at the site of Lees Ferry and looked at the soaring canyon walls and deep river, they didn't just name their campsite in honor of a saint as was their custom. Instead, they called it "San Benito Salsipuedes." *San Benito* referred to the distinctive clothing of penance assigned to persons who had gone astray, and *salsipuedes* meant "get out if you can!" Suffering miserably from cold and heavy rains, so short of food they had to slaughter some of their horses, the men clambered up and down the tortuous cliffs in one futile attempt after another to find a ford. Two of the genízaros failed in an attempt to swim across. Escalante tried to cross with a raft, but the waves repeatedly forced it back to a bank treacherous with quicksand.

On November 7, the little caravan traversed a sandstone slope so steep in one ten-foot section that "it became necessary to cut steps with axes" so the horses could make it down to the river. A short distance downstream, riffles in the water indicated a shallow spot. There the fathers and their companions were finally able to splash across the Colorado, and they headed toward the sere and sandy land of the Hopi Indians—and home.

Sharp spines of cholla cactus evoke varied ordeals of a harsh land. Some Pueblo tribes used them in ceremonies of manhood as implements of pain borne with courage. Domínguez and Escalante met the rigors of their journey armed with profound faith. They considered theirs a divine mission "in behalf of the Light."

I spent a day near the site of the Crossing of the Fathers. The twisting side-canyons where the padres struggled are now accessible by the motorboats that jet across Lake Powell, and I piloted my little boat in shamefaced comfort past the buttes and cliffs that rose from the deep blue waters in a tapestry of color—yellow, apricot, salmon pink, and vivid orange. The impounded waters of Lake Powell have drowned the steps in the sandstone. The course of history had buried the hopes of the padres and they never returned to establish their missions.

Father Domínguez, who had alienated so many churchmen by his critical report, was relegated to a small outpost in northern Mexico; by 1805 he had died in obscurity. Father Escalante served at the Mission of San Ildefonso until he died on a journey in 1780. Miera died in 1785, after completing his map and writing a report to the king, arguing that Spanish colonies in the interior were vital to the defense of California.

But Spain's power was too spent to send settlers along the trail so carefully plotted in the diary. Few Spaniards stopped at the campsites they so carefully named and described. Theirs was the last of the great Spanish explorations. Other men, serving other rulers, would secure the vast lands of the American wilderness. Yet nothing robs the Domínguez-Escalante expedition of the achievement of valiant men challenging the unknown.

WENDELL METZEN

Soaring against the southern sky, gulls evoke the exaltation that naturalist

2 **William Bartram's**

William Bartram found in his travels through the region two centuries ago.

Trail through Nature

By EDWARD O. WELLES, JR.

The fog, swirling over the still river, seemed capable of harboring a world of apparition. I almost expected a slight, gentle man to guide his cypress canoe out of that veiled morning.

William Bartram of Philadelphia, America's first native-born artist-naturalist, explored this river, the Altamaha of Georgia, two centuries ago. Like Mark Catesby before him, John James Audubon after him, he made a deft, enduring cut across the American grain. Sketchbook in hand, he came into a new region to catalogue and celebrate its life, not to conquer it—but for many of his admirers, it is still "Bartram's country" today.

Between 1773 and 1777 he rambled through the Southeast: from Georgia's barrier islands west to the Mississippi, from the savannas of Florida north into the mountains of the Cherokee nation. Along the way he discovered new plant species; drew birds, reptiles, and mammals as well; and wrote extensively of the Indians. He found "an infinite variety of animated scenes." His profuse account of them, his famous *Travels*, appeared in 1791 and swiftly earned him as devoted a following among poets and politicians as it did among naturalists. Printed in four languages, it offered visions of the new land that conveyed his magical detail with his happy enthusiasm.

I had camped on a low bluff by the Altamaha with Richard Trogdon, a Savannah architect. The afternoon before, we had emerged from the backwaters of the river. That primitive zone, with its muddy creeks and honeyed air, was Richard's kind of place. There I sensed his inner clock finding its true rhythm—a man of deliberation, he studied sleeping bags for a year before buying one—while I, a Yankee tense as a spring in the bow of the boat, suspected water moccasins on every overhanging vine-entangled limb.

Now, while I readied our fiberglass canoe, Richard wandered along the eroding bank: "Usually you can find some Indian potsherds—especially after a good rain." I joined him. Moments later, he had four fragments; I had none. He handed me the pieces. Who had once held this clay vessel, here beside this timeless river? Bartram had been here, carried by the "peaceful floods" of the Altamaha, and he had communed with its Indians—"the generous and true sons of liberty."

Perhaps the best testament to a man is not that about him

Fired by a westering sun, the Altamaha River nears its end in the Atlantic Ocean.

Bartram extolled this river's "peaceful floods" in Travels, *his account of his journey through the South between 1773 and 1777. Where the river forms its delta, cord grass sprouts in life-rich salt marsh that flows to the horizon (right).*

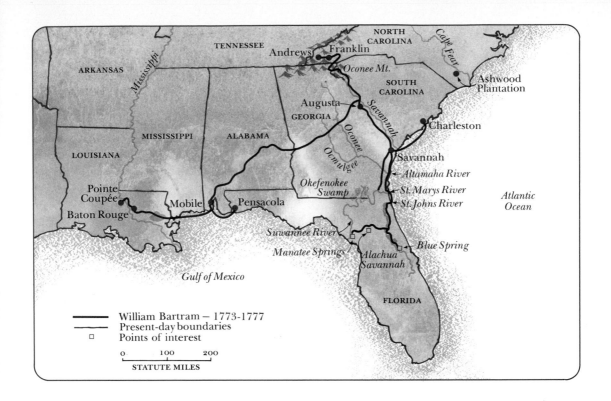

Wanderer's path: For four years Bartram trekked through the South, cataloging whatever claimed his curiosity: the flora and fauna, the face of the land; the "manners, customs and government" of the Indians. His 2,400-mile journey led him west from coastal Georgia to the Mississippi, and north from Florida into the Cherokee nation.

which was, but rather that which endures. In Richard's patience, in his feel for the riverbank, was a facet of Bartram turning to meet the autumn light. For the next two months I would track the naturalist's ghost over its route of long ago and find its life in other kindred spirits, as he did in his own time.

The Philadelphia where William Bartram was born in 1739 was the city of Ben Franklin, philosopher and inventor, a clearing of inquiry in the forest of a new continent. And like Franklin, William was a man of questions. He was also a Quaker, unassuming, but not to be deflected from a chosen path.

He was fortunate in being his father's son. John Bartram, born in the final year of the 17th century, lived through three-quarters of the 18th. Before planting his 287-acre farm, he would contemplate it. He fertilized his fields with a concoction of spring water, ashes, lime, and dung; and his bountiful crops were famous. But he was plowing up native plants, of species he knew little about. The thought troubled him. In 1729 he began cultivating a five-acre botanic garden, one of the first in the colonies.

John's curiosity about his green world was matched an ocean away. In Europe, men of learning wanted American plants for their medicinal value or food; the nobility sought exotic plants for their gardens. A London merchant named Peter Collinson made an agreement with John: John would send him seeds, cuttings, and plants; Collinson would find rich patrons to finance John's botanic excursions into the wilds.

William first accompanied his father in 1753, on a foray into the Catskills. He made drawings of birds that John sent to

White jasmine accents this portrait of Bartram in 1808 by friend and fellow-artist Charles Willson Peale. The flower, an Asian species, suggests the interest in exotic flora which marked the 1700's —and made possible Bartram's career. That century saw the introduction of nearly 500 species of trees and shrubs to Europe from North America. Bartram's father, John, a self-taught botanist, shipped seeds and plants from Philadelphia to patrons in England. In 1753 he began sending drawings by 14-year-old Billy, whose work won him influential admirers. In 1772 a patron offered to pay William for a natural-history survey of the South. Travels, *the result, proved a classic. Until his death in 1823, visitors appeared at his door—often to find him in his garden.*

Collinson. Impressed by their sensitivity, Collinson sent back ink and drawing paper to encourage the gifted teenager.

Young Billy was coming of age; he needed a trade. No one thought art would support him. John consulted Franklin, who offered to teach Billy printing. John thought that a success in this career would demand commercial flair like Franklin's own, as well as "close application." Billy hardly qualified. Still, in 1756 he was apprenticed to a merchant. He spent all his spare time studying natural history. In 1761 he escaped Philadelphia and headed for an uncle's plantation, Ashwood, on the Cape Fear River in North Carolina. There he set up a trading store. He found himself in a dazzling new environment, where all the new creatures needed observing and drawing. The store soon foundered. This experience foreshadowed the next decade.

In 1765 John Bartram traveled in Georgia and Florida as botanist to His Majesty, King George III. William went along. Florida, more tropical than North Carolina and thus more novel, intrigued him more. He remained there and, getting on with the inconvenient business of earning a living, tried his hand at planting rice and indigo. The site he chose on the St. Johns River, part sand and part swamp, seemed more suited to birdwatching. This "frolic," as John called it in chagrin, soon failed, costing the father at least £150. Damaged in health and bankrupt, William returned home in 1767.

Philadelphia didn't improve his fortunes. A stint as a day laborer and another doomed business venture ensued. Despondent and pursued by a small avalanche of debt, William ran away—back to his uncle's plantation. Such "unsteady conduct" distressed Collinson, who was showing William's work to amateur naturalists and possible patrons in Europe.

Among them, luckily, was Dr. John Fothergill, a prominent London physician and collector of exotic plants. He commissioned drawings of shells and turtles. Most significantly, he remained open-minded about his apparently erratic client. In 1772 William abandoned his usual diffidence and proposed a botanic search of Florida. Perhaps in this unusual boldness the doctor sensed the stuff of desperation. After all, the "boy" was now in his early thirties. In a letter to John, Fothergill called it a "pity that such a genius should sink under distress." He assured his "esteemed Friend" that "For his sake, as well as thine, I should be glad to assist him." He consented to fund a long expedition through the southern colonies.

To William the money—£50 a year, plus expenses—and the blank check to wander must have seemed a godsend. On March 20, 1773, his resolve rewarded, he set sail from Philadelphia for Charleston: a voyage southward into spring.

Richard and I launched our canoe into the growing heat of

Wary and alarmed, Bartram meets a menacing Seminole on a woodland path in Georgia, in the spring of 1773. "I resigned myself entirely to the will of the Almighty . . . ," he recalled; "my mind then became tranquil." He offered his hand. After a moment's suspense, the Indian returned the gesture "with dignity in his look and action."

the day, and rode a glassy current into a dazing sun. In the uplands, two rivers—the Ocmulgee and the Oconee—rise and flow south to join. The amplified result is the Altamaha, one of the largest southeastern rivers draining to the Atlantic. Coppery with Georgia Piedmont, it advances to the ocean.

Massive cypress trees occasionally rose from the dense forest walling the river, and lent sudden new proportion to the shore. Of the cypress, Bartram wrote: "Its majestic stature is surprising, and on approaching them, we are struck with a kind of awe.... The delicacy of its colour, and texture of its leaves, exceed every thing in vegetation.... When the planters fell these mighty trees, they raise a stage round them...eight or ten negroes ascend with their axes and fall to work round its trunk." Tannins and oils in the heartwood give the species a strong resistance to rot, a consequent value in the marketplace. The cypress we were seeing were hollow or diseased, unfit for lumber but shelter for small creatures. By their weakness they survived—and aided survival.

Alligators began appearing in the water, little more than eyes and snout visible at the surface. Armored lightning when he lunges into action, the gator can glide along with virtually no ripples of locomotion. He wears the river like a cloak. By noon we had seen half a dozen.

"When I was growing up in Florida," Richard remarked, "it was overpowering to see a gator. They were hunted out so badly." For Bartram, Richard's adjective would have gained meaning. One of the most stirring accounts in *Travels* tells how he was surrounded by voracious alligators on the St. Johns River, "several endeavouring to overset the canoe." He clubbed back two "very large ones" and regained the shore. That evening, gators watched him eat his fresh-caught trout. Their bellowing troubled the night; and Bartram's picture of an onslaught by the "subtle, greedy alligator" keeps the vividness of shock: "Behold him rushing forth from the flags and reeds. His enormous body swells. His plaited tail brandished high, floats upon the lake. The waters like a cataract descend from his opening jaws. Clouds of smoke issue from his dilated nostrils. The earth trembles with his thunder."

Those that we saw seemed shadowy actors in the ecodrama, as quiet as the river itself, symbols of a cosmic order. Like the big cypresses, they belonged here.

Reaching the harbor at Darien by afternoon, we exchanged the canoe for a johnboat with an outboard motor, a flat-bottomed craft better suited to a trip through rougher water to the barrier islands. Richard had to return to Savannah; I would travel with John Crawford.

John's ready smile incandesces from a dark, woolly beard. I would call him a biologist; he just says, "I'm interested in how everything relates out there." That night he would sift a handful of Georgia beach and say, "This sand has seen a lot of mileage." This introduced a brief lecture on how some of its particles

"A Most Blissful Spot"

Mottled by winter, beaded by rain, lily pads float on the waters of the Okefenokee Swamp. When spring returns, their white flowers will cover the dark shallows.

Above, Spanish moss mutes the limbs of a cypress tree rising from the swamp floor— the world of two smaller creatures, a river frog and a rough green snake. Bartram never entered this nearly 700-square-mile area of "terrestrial paradise." He heard from Indians that men got lost here, "involved in perpetual labyrinths."

WENDELL METZEN (ABOVE AND UPPER RIGHT)

probably made up the craggy peaks of the Appalachians about 25 million years ago.

Around Darien, the river casts its burden of Piedmont into delta. Grassy salt marsh, enriched by tidal flux, marches like ripe prairie to all corners of the sky. In this realm lies Broughton Island, where Bartram stopped at a plantation owned by his distinguished friend Henry Laurens of Charleston. Then the land was planted in rice. The ebb and flow of history has returned it to wetland; of the house, only a chimney remains. We could see it, but not make our way to it—the mud seemed ready to swallow us whole, insects to eat us alive.

Next morning we did have a look around. John took out his glasses. As he prepared to put them on they fell in half. He shrugged. Out here, eyes to John Crawford are not the same as eyes to me.

When he was 6 he began playing in a swamp behind his house. Thereafter his mother seldom ventured into his room, deterred by the prodigious ecosystem it contained. At 14 he was lecturing at a nature center in Savannah. At 16 he was a guide to the director of the Pittsburgh zoo for snake-collecting trips; at one time he had 77 snakes, of 38 species. In short, he has credentials worthy of "young Billy Bartram."

We went down to the beach, resurfaced by a nocturnal tide and marked with cryptic symbols. John began to interpret these. A sine wave belonged to a snake; small ridges of sand rose on

Morning sun pierces the live-oak canopy of Florida's Blue Spring Run, whose waters rise from limestone caverns and amble to the St. Johns River.

the outer side of each curve. "This is one way a snake moves; they push off to the side." A trail of skeletal, scrupulous steps recorded a heron: "They're big—probably a great blue." A rabbit had padded across the damp sand, shifting midway from hop to scamper.

We wandered around to the other side of the island, where John crouched under a wax myrtle tree and began chirping. Softly, he named birds as they arrived and perched on the branches: yellowthroat, female American redstart, white-eyed vireo, rufous-sided towhee. This took about a minute. John stood up

Above, a female alligator defends her nest, hissing and snapping at an intruder. This imposing reptile fascinated Bartram. His fanciful depiction of it tells something of the artist: a scientist with a poet's soul.

and dusted sand off his hands: "Four species, that's not bad."

Twenty-three species. That is a conservative figure for the new plants William Bartram discovered. Formally, however, science credits him with only a few of these. Why?

To qualify as a discoverer under the rules of science, you must not only find your creature but also name it properly, describe it technically, and beat any possible rivals into print. Again, Bartram was unlucky.

His specimens were supposed to be forwarded, via Fothergill, for classification by Daniel Solander, a noted Swedish botanist living in London. But Solander, it seems, never got around to them. British expeditions to the South Pacific were bringing in novelties even more startling than those from America. Fothergill died in 1780, Solander two years later. In 1783 Great Britain signed a treaty of peace with the United States, but the old individual ties had been weakened. Bartram's precious finds faded and crumbled an ocean away.

Waiting for expert assistance that never came, hampered by his own considerable fear of criticism, Bartram did not publish *Travels* until 1791. In the four previous years, four major botanic texts appeared—and each one credited someone else with discoveries Bartram had made long since.

What kept Bartram from bitterness was that he was as much poet as scientist. Moreover, "continually impelled by a restless spirit of curiosity," he was deeply devout: "my chief happiness consisted in tracing and admiring the infinite power, majesty and perfection of the great Almighty Creator" whose works he found "most perfect, and every way astonishing!"

This habit of reflection led him to notice ecological patterns as well as sharp detail. In *Travels* he describes a death struggle between a spider and a bumblebee. The "cunning intrepid hunter" stalked the bee with "circumspection" and "perseverance." In the fight, the "rapidity of the bee's wings . . . made them both together appear as a moving vapor." His sympathies with the conquered bee, his intellect tuned to the rhythms of the universe, Bartram reasons at paragraph's end: "and perhaps before night [the spider] became himself, the delicious evening repast of a bird or lizard."

Such musings would probably have disquieted Fothergill. He appealed to his client: Couldn't he be a little more exact, a little more *scientific* in his observations and collections? If William, out in the middle of nowhere, ever received such a pleading missive he probably read it respectfully before filing it deep in pockets already loaded with seeds, shoots, and earth.

Yet it was this same devout, disarming delight in life itself that smoothed Bartram's way on the frontier—and permitted him to keep on botanizing to his patron's advantage. Wandering near the St. Marys River one day, he met an armed Seminole, the first Indian who ever frightened him. Resigning himself

"They struck their jaws together so close to my ears, as almost to stun me," wrote Bartram of an alligator attack on Florida's St. Johns River in early 1774. At right, he clubs the voracious, formidable reptiles away from his cypress canoe. He made his way to shore, where he spent a restive night; ". . . when I arose in the morning, contrary to my expectations, there was perfect peace; very few of them [alligators] to be seen, and those . . . asleep on the shore."

"entirely to the will of the Almighty," Bartram rode up to him and "offered him my hand, hailing him, brother." The Indian, apparently disconcerted, responded in kind, "with dignity in his look and action," and they parted friends. Later Bartram learned that he had met a murderer outlawed by his own people and pledged to kill the first white man he saw.

Bartram was keenly aware that as a white man braving the wilderness he stood in the deepening abyss between one culture which valued the individual's right to own land and a second which had trouble comprehending the very notion. Under the Treaty of Augusta of 1773, the Indians ceded 2,116,298 acres of land in eastern Georgia. In June of that year Bartram accompanied the surveying party through the area.

In a corner of those long-since relinquished lands, in Taliaferro County, Girdwood Macfie lives on a 550-acre farm. This land was granted in December 1773 to James Mendenhall, a second cousin of William Bartram's. Girdwood has lived there for the last 50 years, since his father emigrated to Georgia from his native Scotland via South Africa. A trace of brogue in his speech and veins of rust in a gray beard evoke Girdwood's links to the past.

On a November morning we walked down a narrow dirt road half a mile from his property. It led to Williams Creek, part of the northern boundary of the ceded lands. "In Bartram's day this road started in Augusta and went all the way to the Mississippi River," said Girdwood. We had been passing exact ranks of pines, as if reviewing troops. The pine, with the help of man, has replaced native hardwoods over much of the South: A well-managed pine forest can grow into the realm of commercial profit in 30 years. We followed the road down to the creek.

Girdwood crouched and drew two parallel lines in the clay, a historical map. Cherokee lands lay above the top line, those of the Creeks below the other. Both nations shared rights in the strip of land between. Bartram was an eyewitness to "the great congress" in Augusta when the Creeks—a larger and more powerful federation—forced their rivals to renounce their claim. A Creek warrior stood up "frowning menaces and disdain, fixed his eyes on the Cherokee chiefs, . . . calling them old women, and saying that they [the Creeks] had long ago obliged them to wear the petticoat; a most humiliating (Continued on page 57)

"How Infinite ...Thy Works!"

Charged with vitality, Bartram's vision of nature reflects his interest in each species as a marvel of God's creation. In this tableau he labeled the seed pod of an American lotus (Fig. 1) and the shell of a "large land Snale" (Fig. 2). A clump of flowering blackroot, Indian turnip, and water lettuce almost conceals the snake devouring a kicking frog; a hummingbird perches on a dead shrub and eyes a dragonfly. Such drawings, sent to patrons in England, circulated among connoisseurs; some came to rest in archives and attics, some disappeared. A 59-plate album, made for Bartram's great sponsor John Fothergill, remained unpublished until 1968. It reveals the quality that a discerning critic noticed in Bartram's early work: "a delightful natural freedom."

The Great Alachua-Savana, in East Florida, above 60 miles in circumference.
Near 100 miles W from S. Augustien & 45 miles W. from [...]

"Truly astonishing . . . wild scenes" greeted Bartram at Alachua Savannah in 1774. This panoramic view includes "sprightly deer" and "the beautiful fleet Siminole horse." Other drawings add details from the Florida he found so surprising. In the great yellow bream (left) he saw a "warrior in a gilded coat of mail." He also admired the "sonorous" and "watchful"

sandhill crane (right). The great Mico Chlucco, "King of the Siminoles," wore his mixed European and Indian finery to sit for Bartram's only known portrait; slightly altered by the engraver, it became the frontispiece for Travels.

As dark and as clear as a mountain night, the Suwannee River slides past a wall of cypress.

Bartram judged this spring-fed stream "the clearest and purest of any river I ever saw."

"This Admirable Fountain"

Serenity pervades Florida's Manatee Springs in winter. Nibbling an acorn, a gray squirrel balances on a cypress knee, or gnarled growth from the root. At dusk, an American egret

wades in the outlet stream; leaves of swamp maple hold the fading light. The spring takes its name from the aquatic mammals that ascend the Suwannee River from the Gulf of Mexico to winter in warmer waters. Bartram, visiting in summer, saw only some manatee bones; he noted that the Indians thought them "equal to ivory."

and degrading stroke . . . amidst the laugh and jeers of the assembly. . . ." The Creeks, Bartram concluded, were "arrogant bravos and usurpers" in this episode. Yet, he noted, they were consistently "merciful to a vanquished enemy . . . always uniting the vanquished tribes in confederacy with them; when they immediately enjoy . . . every right of free citizens, and are from that moment united in one common band of brotherhood."

Girdwood began naming trees as we wandered through a brief stand of hardwoods. Sycamore, ash, hickory, sweetgum, hackberry, tulip tree, oak. Then he speculated as to why Bartram's cousin acquired the property six months after the naturalist's visit: "Bartram must have written James and told him he liked the area." (This, characteristically Macfie, was understatement. Bartram exulted over the black-oak forests nearby and worried that nobody would believe his report of trees ten feet in diameter.) We pondered the muddy creek. It was easily fordable, only a figurative boundary. Then we returned up the road, back to where fields abandoned a few decades ago have ceded the land to the pines.

If Bartram had foreseen how tragically the Indians would eventually lose their lands in Georgia, he might never have described this place to his cousin. But at least Girdwood and his wife, Erma, have been good trustees. When Girdwood felt that an adequate history of the area was lacking, he wrote one. When he couldn't find a guide to the local berrying shrubs he compiled one, beginning with a watercolor of each.

Many of Bartram's finest drawings, precise and lyrical and delicately colored, remained unpublished until the 1960's, unnoticed for decades among his patron's papers. Yet his account of his journeying was not wasted. His observations on the Indians form one of the most valuable ethnographic records of the period; he was prepared to report on the reptiles and mammals, rivers and mountains of an ill-charted region.

In January 1777 he returned to his father's house in Philadelphia. Suddenly, that September, his father died. According to a family tradition, the old man's days were shortened by anxiety over "the approach of the royal army, after the battle of Brandywine. As that army had been ravaging various portions of the revolted colonies, he was apprehensive it might also lay waste his darling *garden*, the cherished nursling of half a century."

There, at his birthplace, tending his father's undamaged garden, William Bartram would happily live out his life. He would never marry. His years in the south filled him with a sense of wonder about what lay ten feet from his doorstep—and made him something on the order of a national resource. When the Congress met in Philadelphia, such dignitaries as George Washington, Thomas Jefferson, and James Madison called on him— they were planters, after all.

Visitors arriving without notice on a summer morning might

Storm-felled palms undergo grain-by-grain burial in the sands of Cumberland Island, Georgia. Ocean and wind have crafted this 16-mile-long barrier island within 40,000 years. In March 1774 Bartram walked its "shelly paved sea beach . . . picking up novelties."

cause him some embarrassment, when they found him hoeing the garden in his bare feet, but he would cheerfully share his knowledge of all the plants they wanted to see. One caller, who found him "breaking the clods of earth in a tulip bed," in leather work clothes, wrote that he "entered into conversation with the ease and politeness of nature's noblemen."

President Jefferson, in 1803, offered Bartram the post of botanist on an expedition to the Red River. Citing old age as an excuse, he declined the appointment, as he had already refused a professorship at the University of Pennsylvania. Yet, until his death in 1823, he did some highly significant teaching. Benjamin Smith Barton, a young man keenly interested in natural history, came visiting frequently, and acquired a good deal of information. When his *Elements of Botany* was published, it was largely illustrated by Bartram.

In 1802, an aspiring artist-ornithologist named Alexander Wilson arrived, in need of help. Short of funds, struggling to escape from schoolmastering, he must have made Bartram remember his own youth. Bartram began tutoring him. Wilson confessed on one occasion, "I have murdered your rose....in coloring and shading I got perfectly bewildered." Moreover, he had trouble telling a cardinal from a tanager. But he made rapid

Brown pelican glides over the Georgia marsh. Enriched by some of the highest tides along the southeastern coast, these estuarine waters between the barrier islands and the mainland support a large fish population. The brown pelican,

feeding mainly on mullet and menhaden, obtains its prey in swooping plunges.

progress. With the benefit of Bartram's criticism and patronage, gratefully acknowledged, Wilson produced his *American Ornithology*, a classic that eventually grew to nine volumes.

Travels was published in Philadelphia in 1791. The next year it came out in London; then editions appeared in French, German, and Dutch. In America it sold slowly; its critics among

European scientists found it old-fashioned and too poetic. Nevertheless, Bartram was elected botanist of Philadelphia's Academy of Natural Sciences in 1812, the year of its founding. He had not sought this honor; it acknowledged his status as the grand old man of botany in America.

In the realm of art and literature, book and author would gain a measure of immortality. They would help a pair of poets named Wordsworth and Coleridge summon the muses. The measureless caverns of "Kubla Khan," the water snakes in "The Rime of the Ancient Mariner," and the green savannas of "Ruth" are images which first shone from the pages of *Travels*. Coleridge called the book one of the last "written in the spirit of the old travellers." Some years later, Thomas Carlyle inquired of Ralph Waldo Emerson: "Do you know *Bartram's Travels*? ... [It] has a wondrous kind of floundering eloquence. . . . All American libraries ought to provide themselves with that kind of Books; and keep them as a kind of future *biblical* article."

Verda Horne's small stucco house in Fairhope, Alabama, was full of biblical articles. And she was the besieged librarian. Books filled the living-room shelves, overflowed the office across the hall, and perched on the steps leading to the second floor. "We have four rooms full of books upstairs," she half apologized. She and her husband, Rix, a landscape architect, have lived here beside Mobile Bay for forty years.

Outside, a gray winter evening hurried on as we sat and chatted about Bartram. Verda, a petite and intent woman now in her seventies, has been a teacher all her life—if not always in title, then in spirit. For years she has been active in efforts to establish Bartram's route through Alabama as a hiking trail. She would like to see it used by all sorts of people, not just the devotees of hiking. "We have a poor understanding of trails as a humanizing experience. We only see them as physical adventures."

Since 1975 the idea has grown into a regional concept. The Bartram Trail Conference (a private group), state officials, and federal agencies are working together to extend the trail throughout the South. The enlarged scale of the project has obscured Verda's contribution and those of others, in other states. She interprets this as a sign of progress: "Nobody on God's green earth will care who started the Bartram Trail. They'll worry about whether or not there is one."

After all, she points out, if anyone "started" it, it was Bartram himself: "We're all following his trail."

As yet, only small segments of Bartram's route exist as established trail. In late October I was on one such fragment in the Nantahala Mountains of North Carolina. One day the Bartram Trail will wend south from here, down through the Georgia forest and over into South Carolina, through Oconee State Park. On Oconee mountain, one distant spring, Bartram was so rapt by a "view inexpressibly magnificent and comprehensive" that he

Overleaf: Bartram rides into a glade near the summit of Oconee mountain in South Carolina on a spring day in 1776. He holds the blossom of a Carolina rhododendron, a species he has just discovered, but other flowers capture his attention: the flame azalea, first recorded by his father and himself. William alone found at least 23 new plant species; the Seminoles called him Puc-Puggy, the Flower Hunter.

almost overlooked "a new species of Rhododendron foremost in the assembly of mountain beauties." (These flowers included the lovely "flaming azalea" that he and his father had discovered on their trip together.) He did his best to convey a scene "infinitely varied, and without bound" in full splendor: "The mountainous wilderness . . . down to the region of Augusta, appearing regularly undulated as the great ocean after a tempest . . . the nearest ground to me of a perfect full green; next more glaucous, and lastly almost blue as the ether with which the most distant curve of the horizon seems to be blended."

With Ed Moss, a friend from Washington, D. C., I had followed this brief trace west from the town of Franklin up the rising ridgeline toward Wayah Bald. Late on the second day, up around 5,000 feet, we began feeling the mountain's steepness. My pack, an agglomeration of lightweight synthetics, took on the feel of pig iron. It was time to find a place to camp.

I saw what looked like a footpath leading off the trail. Ed was skeptical, and the thicket of rhododendron I was soon staggering through quickly banished this "footpath" to the outer provinces of the imagination.

But moments later we came crashing out into a magnificent open forest, and stood stunned. Columnar hardwoods—oaks, maples, tulip trees—rose to an aery ceiling. Strewn around like massive figures of sculpture were those that had gone before them. The elements in disassembling them worked rich designs in their trunks, a labor which seemed the antithesis of decay. Down where the forest floor disappeared back into a grove of rhododendron, water came springing out of the mossy earth and trickling over rocks. We would call this glade home for the next three days.

We had reached a magical place. This niche in the mountainside, by its utter separateness, gave time a chance to double back on itself. I could not escape the conviction that Bartram in person would come wandering into camp around sundown, so we would be three around the fire that night. I knew that he had died one sultry July morning a century and a half ago; he had finished writing a description of a plant, wandered outside, and fallen instantly dead in his beloved garden.

But I could echo the tribute paid him by one of Georgia's leading naturalists in 1854, one who traced his route early enough to find "every thing exactly as he reported." John Eatton Le Conte wrote: "Mr. Bartram was a man of unimpeached integrity and veracity, of primeval simplicity of manners and honesty unsuited to these times, when such virtues are not appreciated." How many admirers, I thought, appreciate them now.

"Of the first order for beauty and fragrance"—Bartram's painting of the Franklinia, considered his finest botanical illustration, supports his praise. He and his father found

EDMUND B. GILCHRIST, JR.; COURTESY PENNSYLVANIA HORTICULTURAL SOCIETY

this extremely rare tree in 1765 and named it in honor of their friend Benjamin Franklin. A Franklinia still blooms in the Bartrams' garden in Philadelphia, long a shrine for botanists, today a city park.

Franklinia alatamaha. A beautiful flowering Tree.

discovered growing near the banks of the R. Alatamaha in Georgia.

Will.ᵐ Bartram. Delin.
1788.

Early-morning fog drifts through Appalachian valleys in Harlan County, Kentucky.

3 Daniel Boone: Beyond

Through nearby Cumberland Gap, Boone and other pioneers crossed into western lands.

the Settlements By RICHARD T. SALE

In June of 1820, the painter Chester Harding came to the trading town of St. Charles, a cluster of houses on the Missouri River. He rode on for twenty miles, getting directions with difficulty, until he reached a log blockhouse deep in the woods. Hitching up his horse, he went to the door.

An extraordinary scene met his eyes. An old man lay on a bunk near the hearth, roasting a strip of deer meat wrapped on a ramrod. He turned the venison at the crackling blaze, added salt and pepper. Though decrepit, he was quite striking: a face with

His injured dog held before him, Dr. Thomas Walker rides through Cumberland Gap. A land speculator, he located the pass in 1750 on a surveying trip. Years later, Daniel Boone led settlers through the gap into Kentucky—and it became part of the Boone legend.

intensely blue eyes, almost piercingly stern; a hooked nose and high cheekbones; the mouth a bit sunk with age but still held firm. The old fellow wore his hair in a knot behind his head.

This singular creature was Daniel Boone, living in a cabin built years earlier. Daniel was 85 years old, so infirm, says tradition, that someone had to support his head while Harding toiled at his likeness. Patriotic citizens had commissioned the work, to the family's surprise. Three months later, the portrait completed, Boone died, one of the most famous men in America.

"It was on the first of May, in the year 1769, that I resigned my domestic happiness for a time, and left my family and peaceable habitation on the Yadkin River, in North-Carolina, to wander through the wilderness of America, in quest of the country of Kentucke. . . ."

Such are the words of Daniel Boone as reported in the book that was the chief instrument of his fame. Entitled *The Discovery, Settlement and present State of Kentucke,* by John Filson, it was published in 1784 and quickly translated into French and German. Boone's "autobiography," an appendix to the book, appears to be Filson's work-up of notes from an interview with Boone, and it paints a lurid picture. At first, Kentucky is "an howling wilderness, the habitation of savages and wild beasts," rank with violence that "shed the blood of the innocent." And then Boone came—a soldier of Providence, ordained by the Almighty to advance the civilization and the extension of his country.

The book delighted its audience here and abroad. Americans relished its patriotism. Europeans had made the philosophy of Jean-Jacques Rousseau all the rage: The primitive had become the ideal, the contented self-sufficiency of the "natural man." Boone seemed a hero for all readers.

The Kentucky countryside seemed pretty tame as I first drove through it. Try as I would to see it with the eyes of Boone's contemporaries, it was hardly "dark and bloody ground." Meadowlike country surrounds Louisville, but by the time I was near Boonesborough, the road wound through lumpish, heavily wooded hills. This is raw country in November, all loneliness and solitude. The car passed dark stands of thick woods.

Next morning the land was white. Snow blew across the road, twisting like scarves as the wind lashed it into a blizzard.

"You can't get lost in Kentucky," said the fellow in the gas station. "Not any more, not in our day and age."

On one of his prolonged hunting trips, even Boone, an expert traveler, was lost for three days. Not that he admitted it. With a stout pride—and perhaps a flicker of wit—he conceded to Harding that "I was *bewildered* once for three days."

I was feeling more bewildered all the time. But the mechanic was right. In our day you can turn up a wrong road, but you always know vaguely where you are. Suddenly, in the gray-white blur, lights of a car ahead of me flashed bright red. I stopped, got out. Talking to a party of duck hunters, I found that far ahead a huge tractor-trailer lay on its side blocking our way. Boonesborough would have to wait; I turned back, to discuss its hero with authorities on his career.

"I've never read a single book or article about Daniel Boone that was really good," said the noted historian Charles Gano Talbert. He is author of an admirable biography of Boone's contemporary and comrade-in-arms Benjamin Logan. Like most scholars, Dr. Talbert grows impatient with the popular myths: that Boone was the first explorer to set foot in Kentucky, that he was the founder of Boonesborough, that he was the unsociable loner who brought civilization to the land west of the Allegheny Mountains. Dr. Talbert's own teacher, Dr. Thomas D. Clark, says, "every author tries to make the man live up to the myth."

"All the writers try to do is stick in all the old unproven stories," Mrs. Audrea McDowell told me at the Filson Club. This is a gaunt old red-brick building in Louisville, a center of scholarship, with well-equipped reading rooms. For years she had worked with her husband, the late Robert Emmett McDowell, on a definitive Boone biography. Bales of notes were gathered; he signed a publisher's contract; he completed a first chapter—and then he died, leaving a mass of crowded files. Mrs. McDowell knows this material well. About Filson she was most emphatic.

"Filson was a publicity agent, a PR man for real estate interests in Kentucky," she said bluntly. He owned more than 12,000 acres himself, and she thinks he wrote to lure large numbers of settlers and thus increase the value of his own holdings. "Look," she pointed out, "Boone's letters are practically illiterate; he could hardly have come up with an autobiography like that."

In a letter of 1786 he asked for "a Nother Copy" of a lost paper and promised to send his work "to the ofis a medetly," signing himself "your omble Sarvent."

By contrast, Filson's prose glitters with fake gems. He has Boone musing sagely that "Felicity, the companion of content, is rather found in our own breasts than in the enjoyment of external things." Or calling some wilderness mountains "the ruins, not of Persepolis or Palmyra, but of the world!"

Mrs. McDowell concluded, "I think Filson's book contains about as much truth as a commercial brochure of that kind would have today."

For inquirers like the McDowells and Dr. Talbert, the search for a believable Daniel Boone is a saga of telephone calls to county courthouses, of trying to locate old records, of interviews, of hunting down books long out of print, of peering at magnifying screens that display the cramped, botched contents of microfilmed documents. One student compares it to "trying to track last year's buck through this year's fallen leaves." The facts are hard to find and often harder to check, and a lie or misstatement once set in circulation is frequently more entertaining than the correction which seems to be so colorless and to come so late.

Certificate of survey, legal in form but shaky in spelling, remains as one of the few original documents by Daniel Boone. As a deputy surveyor, he drafted it to describe property in "Burbin" County, Kentucky. His knowledge of the land proved valuable to investors. As early as

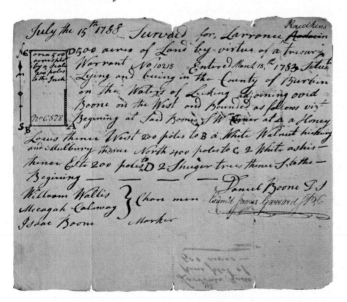

1763, Richard Henderson of North Carolina hired him to scout little-known frontier areas. Boone staked many claims for himself and others, eventually losing most of them in lawsuits.

Boone at 85, reddish hair gone white, keeps a rough-hewn dignity in artist Chester Harding's copy of the portrait he painted in 1820—the only likeness from life.

Daniel was born to Sarah and Squire Boone, a Quaker weaver who left Devon, England, to settle in Pennsylvania. His means were small, but his family eventually numbered 11 children. Daniel, the sixth son, was born in Berks County in 1734.

We know next to nothing of his childhood and youth, but it cannot have differed greatly from the life Abraham Lincoln lived as a boy. As Bertrand Russell wrote, "Hard work, traditions of Indians, solitude, and the silence of the forest made up his environment." That, plus guns, hunting, and an endless succession of farm chores.

An account of 18th-century settlement life by the great historian Francis Parkman conveys the essentials: a cluster of barns, outbuildings and sheds, then the houses—the whole a tiny scar in the dark pelt of the woods. It was, of course, the promise of owning land that helped draw settlers like Squire Boone to America in the first place.

Boone's father represents a significant class, the small freeholder. The ideal of the time was that of the self-reliant man, and the quickest way a man could prosper was by acquiring land. They were a tough, hardy group. Their success in a hostile environment made them loath to admit that anyone was better than they. It was men like Boone's father who would be the strongest backers of Jeffersonian democracy.

What many of them could *not* do, it seems, was stay put. As the land filled up, and the price or rent for it rose, these men moved inland, where land was cheaper.

By 1750 when Daniel was 16, Squire Boone was at odds with other Friends; two of his children married "out of Meeting." Drawn by rumors of cheap land, he picked up and moved southwest, down the "great valley road" of the Shenandoah to North Carolina. In the fall of 1751 he reached the Yadkin valley, where an Indian trading path met the road. He chose the crest of a hill, cleared a plot, and built a crude cabin. The town of Salisbury was 12 miles away; to the west was Indian country, and beyond the mountains lay territory claimed by France. Already France and England, the two great powers in North America, were contending for what only one would be able to possess.

What was at stake was an empire. The French allied themselves with the Indians of the Ohio country. The English allotted grants to the newly organized Ohio and Loyal land companies. Both companies were to explore the west, determine trade routes and areas for settlement, and deal with the Indians. Both needed good agents and they got them, the Ohio Company taking on Christopher Gist while the Loyal turned to Dr. Thomas Walker.

Gist's journeys took him through western Pennsylvania, Kentucky, and Ohio. On each trip he made careful maps. On the same kind of mission, Dr. Walker made a single great discovery.

He had set out from Albemarle County on March 6, 1750, with five other men and two packhorses. Following riverbanks and creeks, buffalo roads and Indian paths, he reached a gap in the mountains: "This Gap may be seen at a considerable distance," he noted. Here was the looked-for breach in the Alleghenies, the route for a stream of settlers after the Revolution, the pass famous as Cumberland Gap. Daniel Boone would not even see it for 19 years, but it would become part of the Boone legend.

Clashes in the Ohio region flared into war; in 1755, the English decided to strike the French in force. The army of Maj. Gen. Edward Braddock was to move northwest from Virginia and take Fort Duquesne, on the site of present-day Pittsburgh. Braddock's disaster is famous. Ambushed in the woods, many of his men were killed in their tracks and the remainder fled. Among the survivors were George Washington, Christopher Gist, a guide named John Findlay, and a perfectly obscure wagoner called Daniel Boone.

The next summer Boone married 17-year-old Rebecca Bryan, a tall brunette who would give him ten children and with whom he would share his colorful, irregular life. He bought a home place in 1759, paying his father £50 for 640 acres of Yadkin land. He had farmed before the Braddock campaign and he would try it from time to time all his life, selling and buying cabins and plots, moving to new counties, but somehow never really able to establish himself. No sooner had a field been cleared, a cabin put up, corn planted, than Boone was off with his packhorses and rifle, disappearing into the distant mountains.

Lured by tales of Kentucky, Boone left North Carolina for the "hunters' paradise" in 1769. Later, he blazed

the Wilderness Road through Cumberland Gap. In his quest for promising land, he explored east and west of the Alleghenies. As a captive of the Shawnee, he passed several months in Ohio. Boone spent his last years near St. Charles, Missouri.

"He cast his eyes towards the residence of a family always dear to him—he felt the pang which absence gave," sighs an 1812 biographer. This figure of Boone the reluctant wanderer is part of popular legend. So is the theme of Boone as a man averse to society of any kind. This appears as early as 1786, and gains popularity in the 19th century. An 1816 article says, "he might have accumulated riches as readily as any man in Kentucky; but he *prefers the woods,* where you see him in the dress of the roughest, poorest hunter."

Boone was among the poorest, but it was his neglect of his finances that caused him to be so. In 1763 he got so far behind in paying his debts that some of the leading citizens of Salisbury brought suit against him, and he escaped real trouble only because the most influential citizen of all stepped forward to take up his defense. Attorney Richard Henderson had by then climbed to the top of his town's tree.

Like his ambitious peers, Henderson was not only eager to secure land but also anxious to keep his activities secret. In Virginia, Thomas Jefferson, Patrick Henry, and George Washington were all involved in speculation schemes at one time or another. In 1767 Washington urged his backwoods agent William Crawford to look for a fertile tract without alarming the Indians, the colonial officials, or commercial rivals—"by a Silent management . . . under the pretence of hunting other Game. . . ."

Land hunger worked on differing scales—a small scale, with Squire Boone. In Henderson it took on scope—he dreamed of a private empire. Daniel Boone, it seems, was not content with the first and not disciplined enough to carry off the second. He was a good example for the frontier observation that the men who wandered the wilderness did the least to develop it. Backwoodsmen like Boone broke open the new routes to wealth, but it was other men who used them to advantage: men of more sober mind, more consistent effort, more abundant means. Men like Richard Henderson.

Henderson knew Boone as a hunter, traveler, surveyor, waybreaker, road cutter. If Boone lacked cash to pay for Henderson's legal services, he could pay in woodsmanship.

By 1768, Boone had tried a number of things and failed at all of them. Neglecting his debts, he had gone off to Florida; and tradition says he bought a house and lot in Pensacola in 1763. When Rebecca—for once—refused to move, he abandoned the notion. He spent a few years of obscurity exploring eastern Tennessee. In 1767 he made his first attempt to enter Kentucky. Setting out in the autumn, he was snowed in, found the tangles of laurel impenetrable, and came home, the trip a fiasco.

In the fall of 1768, as the hues of squash and pumpkin began to fleck the leaves, a visitor came to Boone's door—and changed his life. Dressed in coarse clothes, leading packhorses for trade, the man was none other than John Findlay, Boone's fellow veteran from the Braddock campaign. Findlay had lived in Kentucky as early as 1752, among the Shawnee, and wanted to return there. Like Boone, he was out of pocket.

Many historians think Henderson was a secret sponsor when Boone and four other adventurers set out from Salisbury for Kentucky on May 1, 1769—with Findlay as guide. The trip turned sour. Findlay's health broke down. The party was attacked by the Shawnee, who stole the pelts Boone had gathered for sale. Yet Boone remained to roam the area for two years—probably spying out the land for Henderson.

As Robert Emmett McDowell pointed out in an article, Kentucky was already "comparatively well known" for a region without white settlers. Two other expeditions were traveling there in 1769; trappers had already made hundreds of visits.

Boone undertook to guide a party of would-be settlers, including his own family, in 1773. Not far from the Cumberland Gap some of them were surprised by hostile Shawnee. Boone's eldest son, James, and the son of Captain William Russell from Virginia, were both wounded and spent their last agonized moments under the Indians' knives. A black slave, who hid nearby, heard their screams and reported their fate. The family reaction to this tragedy can be imagined from the "autobiography's" words on the loss of yet another son: "I cannot reflect upon this dreadful scene, but sorrow fills my heart."

Despite such risks, the race to settle Kentucky was on by March 1775. James Harrod, from the Monongahela region, had founded the first town the previous summer. Unfazed, Henderson acted with decision. Using Boone to gather the Cherokee,

whose claims to the land were dubious at best, Henderson met in council with them for several days. At the end he had purchased twenty million acres of Kentucky for items worth several thousand pounds—pots and pans, tools and sundry goods.

"There is something in that Affair which I neither understand, nor like, and wish I may not have cause to dislike it worse as the Mistery unfolds," huffed George Washington. But Henderson had his private colony, Transylvania, and he promptly sent Boone with an armed party to take possession. Near the Kentucky River, a Shawnee raid stunned the party. Two men were killed; others began to turn back. Henderson, far to the rear, began to fear that Boone, too, would retreat.

At peace in the woods of Kentucky, Daniel Boone sprawls on a deerskin and sings to himself and his dog. Startled hunters who overheard him made the incident a vivid anecdote for the Boone tradition.

A Hunter's World

Antlers in July velvet, a white-tailed buck forages in Dolly Sods Wilderness, West Virginia. Fleabane blooms near Cumberland Gap. In such a world Daniel Boone hunted, trapped, and explored.

N.G.S. PHOTOGRAPHER BRUCE DALE

ANIMALS ANIMALS/© AMIL MYSHIN (OPPOSITE)

DR. E. R. DEGGINGER, BRUCE COLEMAN INC. (ABOVE)

Wilderness creatures—like this raccoon—became part of the Boone myth. Artists have often portrayed him wearing a coonskin cap, headgear he heartily disliked.

Eerie stillness warns of a November storm in Kentucky's Rockcastle River gorge. In similar

weather Boone hunted here—today the area belongs to a national forest named in his honor.

He needn't have. Boone resolutely kept his men together, chose a site, and went to work building a fort. Unfortunately, as Mrs. McDowell points out, "he put the thing right in the middle of a floodplain by the Kentucky River." Indians on the nearby heights could fire down into the cluster of cabins. When Henderson arrived, he ordered a new fort built on a new site upriver.

Today, a restored monument, the capital of Henderson's colony stands lifeless. On a winter day you walk up a steep slope with brown leaves crackling underfoot. You hear water trickling somewhere, the only sound. Suddenly, through the bare trees, you see a dull shape with two flatheaded towers at each end. You get closer, and the pattern of the logs starts to come clear: a stronghold, important only for the history books.

Ironically, the first deadly assault on the place came not from Indians but from the Virginia legislature. For months it debated the case, Henderson trying to obtain ratification of his purchase and Jefferson, Henry, and George Rogers Clark trying to render it null. The blow fell in December of 1776. Kentucky became a county of Virginia, itself now a free and independent state. For compensation, the state gave Henderson 200,000 acres of very fine land. And Boone? Having the capital named Boonesborough would be his sole reward. He lost the prime acreage Henderson had promised him for his efforts, but he did become a captain in the Virginia militia.

As Filson gives the story, Boone never once refers to the Revolutionary War as a matter of high strategy or statecraft or diplomacy. He mentions "his Britannick Majesty" in passing, but he tells only of Indian raids.

These were frequent. One produced a cherished story. In the summer of 1776, three Boonesborough girls were kidnapped by the Shawnee, Jemima Boone and two daughters of Colonel Richard Callaway, Betsey and Fanny. The quick-witted girls left broken twigs, bits of clothing, and other signs to mark a trail. Boone and a party of men hunted the Indians down and rescued the girls unharmed.

Kentucky was highly vulnerable. There were only three American "towns" in 40,000 square miles, tiny specks within forests broken only by rivers and creeks. Control of the Ohio valley rested with three English forts, Kaskaskia, Vincennes, and Detroit. George Rogers Clark assembled a small force of frontiersmen and set out to capture them. Clark would take the valley and his would be the major campaign of Kentucky's war.

If Boonesborough was but a sidelight of the Revolution, for Boone himself it meant some of the most dramatic—and controversial—events of his life. On New Year's Day, 1778, he set out for the salt springs called the Blue Licks, about 70 winding miles away, taking some 30 men to make salt for the garrisons.

Salt was vital on the frontier. It not only preserved food but also often disguised a tainted flavor. Boiling down the natural

George Rogers Clark, a hero of the Revolution in the West, appears in the solitude of command in a portrait by Howard Pyle. Leading an "army" of 175 men, he captured Kaskaskia and Vincennes, key British posts in the Ohio country. At these bases Indians received weapons for their attacks on American settlements. While Clark waged his far-ranging campaign, pioneers like Boone fought to defend isolated little forts from Indian onslaughts.

brine was simple but tedious. By February 7 the party had made 300 bushels and Boone had ridden off to check some beaver traps. As one of his men, Joseph Jackson, recalled six decades later, scouts from a sizable party of Shawnee were out in a heavy snowstorm. They met Boone leading "his horse loaded with buffalo meat . . . and it was still snowing so fast, that they got within thirty steps of him before he saw them."

Boone abandoned his loaded horse and ran for it, but after a long chase through the forest the Indians had him outflanked at easy range. Exhausted, he surrendered.

Next morning, the men at the licks saw him approaching and thought he was bringing reinforcements. When they recognized the men behind him as Indians, they grabbed for their guns but he shouted, "Don't fire! If you do, all will be massacred." At his order, his men gave up.

The Shawnee took their captives, by a long march through the snow, to their towns beyond the Ohio, then delivered Boone and about ten others to the English at Detroit on March 30. There Boone convinced the British commander, Henry Hamilton, that Kentucky might return to its old allegiance. He promised to arrange the surrender of Boonesborough.

Refusing Hamilton's offer to buy Boone for £100, the great chief Blackfish took his star prisoner back to the Shawnee town of Old Chillicothe. "I spent my time as comfortably as I could expect," Boone says in Filson; "was adopted, according to their custom, into a family where I became a son. . . ."

Custom called for a ritual bathing of the prisoner, who was then given new clothes, and the purpose was more functional than sentimental.

"Adoption very often meant the replacement of a dead son," explains Dr. Erminie Wheeler-Voegelin, an authority on the

Shawnee. "And thereafter a captive's white blood was ignored. It had been washed away."

Boone bided his time in captivity. To the disgust of his fellow prisoners, he seemed to like Indian life. I'm reminded of the passage in *Huckleberry Finn:* "It was kind of lazy and jolly. . . . It was pretty good times up in the woods there, take it all around." Mrs. McDowell says, "What is mind-boggling when you study Boone's life is not the way he fought Indians but the way he got along with them." She thinks his Quaker background is important in this—"The Quakers went out of their way to do right by the Indians." And Dr. Talbert adds, "I think he thought a bit like an Indian himself."

Stealthily as any warrior, Boone escaped on June 16 and reached Boonesborough on June 20 after covering 160 miles. On the way his horse had broken down, near the Ohio River. He warned Colonel Callaway and the rest to expect a strong war party in pursuit. Yet nothing much happened. The water supply was low; the men began to dig a well, but didn't complete it. Slowly, two new blockhouses were built, but left unroofed. Perhaps the explanation lies in a pioneer explorer's comment that frontier settlers often showed "a thorough aversion to labor."

Ten summer weeks went by. Reinforcements came in: all of fifteen men.

On the morning of September 7, the settlers saw Indians arriving in strength. A truce was declared, and Captain Boone went out to meet Chief Blackfish. Blackfish produced a letter from Henry Hamilton, demanding the surrender Boone had promised at Detroit. Hamilton had sent 400 warriors and a dozen whites to make sure Boone closed the deal. A council was held in the fort. Supposedly Boone set forth the advantages of surrender. Callaway and the others flatly refused to give up.

Remote in the wilds, Boonesborough stood vulnerable. In 1775, Richard Henderson sent Boone to build it. At left, a drawing made in 1900—after Henderson's own plan—portrays it before its major siege, in 1778. Today, as if seen by an enemy scout, a reconstruction looms beyond leafless branches of a shrub called burning bush.

"Well, well," Boone allegedly remarked, "I'll die with the rest."

Negotiations outside the stockade dragged on and on. It seems that on the fifth day, when the settler-officers still refused all demands, Blackfish tried to capture them by treachery as they were shaking hands. A short and terrible struggle followed. Men stood face to face in scuffling knots; they struck, clawed, kicked, pounded at each other. Then the settlers broke free and dashed for the fort.

The siege lasted more than a week, a frontier classic of murky woods, freckled sunlight, sniper's bullets pinging against

the walls, the reek of wood smoke and gunpowder, frantic shouts. One day the defenders heard a new sound, of woodchopping, from men out of sight below the riverbank. Then the river suddenly turned from blue to muddy tan. Led by a European officer, the Indians were trying to tunnel into the fort. Mizzling rain set in as the settlers began to countermine. The rain increased, driving like volleys of arrows. Night came on and the rain continued, lightning making muffled flashes in cloud.

At dawn the sound of digging had ceased. The soggy ground had collapsed the tunnels. The disgusted Indians had gone.

Filson recorded one detail that sounds authentic: "we picked up one hundred and twenty-five pounds weight of bullets, besides what stuck in the logs of our fort."

And then Daniel Boone faced a court-martial, at Logan's Fort. Colonel Callaway brought grave charges against him. That he voluntarily surrendered his men at the Blue Licks. That he promised Hamilton to surrender the people of Boonesborough to be taken to Detroit. That he weakened the garrison when an Indian army was expected. That he took officers of the fort beyond the protection of the guns of its defenders, on the pretense of making peace with Blackfish.

Of all the episodes in Boone's life, the details of his court-martial lie farthest from the reach of hard evidence. Only one eyewitness account survives, and it does not even name the members of the court. His defense is known, generally, a ready answer for each charge.

By surrendering the salt-makers he had diverted the Indians from an attack on Boonesborough. Yes, a fellow prisoner had heard him tell Hamilton he would surrender the garrison; that

Overleaf: Freshly bathed, Boone waits to receive Indian clothing in a Shawnee adoption ritual performed at a town called Old Chillicothe, near the modern Xenia, Ohio. In

KARL BODMER AND JEAN-FRANÇOIS MILLET; S. P. AVERY COLLECTION, PRINTS DIVISION, NEW YORK PUBLIC LIBRARY (ABOVE AND OPPOSITE)

was a lie told to deceive the enemy. He took men from the fort to observe the Indians. He had urged a parley with Blackfish, but only to gain time for reinforcements to arrive.

Boone was acquitted. Mrs. McDowell thinks it highly unlikely that Boone was disloyal, adding, "I don't think he had a political bone in his body." Apparently Callaway and Benjamin Logan were not pleased with the outcome. But the exact truth? The records of the trial mysteriously disappeared, no one is quite sure when, probably in an effort to protect Boone's historical reputation by keeping the case from general knowledge. The idea of Boone as disloyal was too shocking to be allowed.

"Although he lived to be 86 years old, Boone did little that added to his stature or historical importance in his later life," says scholar Marshall Fishwick. Boone did acquire land, but as early as 1785 he faced the first of a series of lawsuits that eventually deprived him of all his holdings.

His postwar career as a surveyor was an unhappy joke. Unreliable in details, never punctual, he had to work in a land-recording system that was a haphazard muddle. In Kentucky,

February 1778, a Shawnee party captured Boone and other men making salt near the Licking River; they took ransom for some, adopted others. The ceremony offered a way of replacing dead relatives, and suggests that the Indians held Boone in high regard. As a prisoner, he shrewdly respected Shawnee custom. In June, he escaped and hurried to warn the people of Boonesborough of a Shawnee attack.

Snow-laden trees border Licking River near the site of Boone's capture by the Shawnee. After his death, stories grew around his colorful and complex life. Below, a carving on a

JOHN AGNONE, N.G.S. STAFF

monument to Boone in Frankfort, Kentucky, depicts him in his legendary role as an Indian fighter. In fact, the frontier hero shared with the Indians a common spirit, a relationship of respect born in the wilderness.

surveyor's claims overlapped like shingles; titles and deeds were often in doubt. Impatient with paperwork, he often failed to complete it and then sold land he did not legally own. In ten years' time, Boone lost not only all of his own best lands but also those of the people who had employed him as their surveyor.

His mail began to grow bitter. "The thousand acres warrant that I first put in your hands cost me dear . . . ," wrote one Charles Yancey in 1796. Boone reminded the Governor of Kentucky that he had never been paid for his "trubel" in cutting the Wilderness Road in 1775; he never was. By 1798 Boone's creditors had him at bay. In that year alone 10,000 acres of his land were sold for back taxes. "Before he left Kentucky . . . ," wrote Robert McDowell, "he was probably one of the most cordially hated men in the state."

In 1788, he moved to the Kanawha valley, in what is now West Virginia. About ten years later, he moved to St. Charles, then under the rule of his Catholic Majesty, the King of Spain. He became the presiding magistrate of the district, and he had wife and children and grandchildren around him.

Recently I visited there. Spring was just beginning, a vast, momentous stirring. Trees on the rolling hills were bare at first, but the air grew balmy and the stark branches began to blur in a haze of green. I wandered into the woods, which were quiet and sunlit. They bordered a clean, shallow river, cluttered with pale boulders.

Boone's is an elusive trail. As one researcher says, "he moves like mist on a mountain river; he's always just over the next hill, and you can't catch up with him." But here . . . "So he lived here," I thought. Apparently he was happy. I think his irresponsible streak went with his contentment, a love of idleness with a joyous energy, an absorption in the moment without the tiresome prudence that always has to be looking ahead.

He lived out a long life, hunting, fishing, gradually growing blind. He lost land the Spanish authorities had given him when it came under American rule, but his children still had plenty. He had become a hero of the frontier in his own time; the future would hail him as "Prince of the Pioneers . . . Founder of Boonesborough . . . Foster-Father of Kentucky . . . peerless Pilot of the Republic . . . divinely ordained to settle the Wilderness."

When Filson was mentioned, Boone would say stoutly, "All true! Every word true! Not a lie in it!" And perhaps at the end it seemed to the old woodsman that all the legends were true.

Barrier of snow and stone, the Rockies beyond the Athabasca River Valley challenged

4 Mackenzie and Thompson

early explorers, who dared crossings even in winter in search of new fur-trade routes.

in Canada's Vastness

By JOHN HESS

SIR THOMAS LAWRENCE; THE NATIONAL GALLERY OF CANADA, OTTAWA

*Alexander Mackenzie strikes a proud pose in a portrait
painted in 1800. Discoverer of the Mackenzie River, he won
fame as the first white man to cross the continent north of
Mexico. Returning to London, the youthful explorer appeared
as a man of fashion—a success in the Royal Court as well as
the Rockies. Shortly after the publication of his volume*
Voyages, *King George III knighted him for his exploits.*

J ust once, in years of risk and hardship, two of Canada's greatest explorers met in the field. David Thompson, "unknown to the world," proudly recorded in his journal for May 1798 a handsome compliment from Alexander Mackenzie, the "celebrated traveller."

"Upon my report to him of the surveys I had made . . . he was pleased to say I had performed more in ten months than he expected could be done in two years."

Mackenzie had earned renown leading an expedition north from Lake Athabasca, along the river that now bears his name, to the Arctic Ocean. He went some 1,500 miles downstream in 40 days, fighting his way back against the current in only 59. And in the ten months singled out for praise, Thompson had traveled more than 4,000 miles through ill-known country, mapping much of present-day Manitoba and Saskatchewan. He had crossed the plains to the upper Missouri River and explored the sources of the Mississippi, working through the gales and blizzards of winter, making astronomical observations when storms permitted.

I gained my own respect for the scope of the northern wilderness in comparative luxury, on U. S. Air Force search-and-rescue flights in Alaska in the 1950's. Even now, when a plane goes off the radar screen and breaks radio contact, it may be lost for months—or forever. Flying those long searches, you learn the vastness of the land, and even in the comfort of a modern base you sense the strain of the slow winter.

During his third year in the north, at the fur-trade base called Cumberland House, 16-year-old David Thompson found himself playing checkers with the devil: "his features and color were those of a Spaniard, he had two short black horns on his forehead . . . his countenance mild and grave; we began playing, played several games and he lost every game, kept his temper, but looked more grave; at length he got up, or rather disappeared." Deeply impressed by this eerie experience, young Thompson decided never again to play a game of chance or skill. Apparently it never occurred to him to think of his dangerous journeys as hazards of that kind.

In the winter of 1793-1794, after his epic journey across the

Fired by his vision of a passage to the Pacific, Mackenzie followed the river that now bears his name—only to find that it led to the Arctic. Disappointed but not discouraged, he mounted a second expedition in 1793,

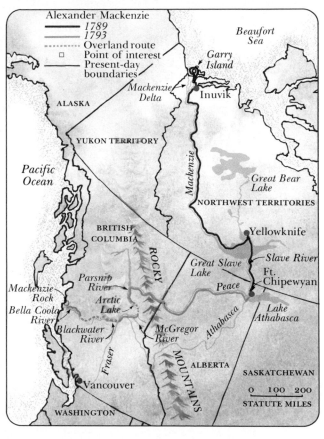

reaching the coast after a tortuous journey that took him 1,200 miles in 74 days. Despite his failure to establish a profitable trade route, he opened a vast new area to the fur companies.

H. A. OGDEN, "AT THE PORTAGE"; PUBLIC ARCHIVES OF CANADA

Fortunes in Fur

"CONTINENTAL"
COCKED HAT.
(1776)

Valued for its fur, the beaver—Castor canadensis—lured explorers into the Canadian wilderness. A fashion for beaver hats (right) in Europe fueled a booming trade in beaver pelts. Hatmakers removed the soft underfur, which pressed easily into a high-grade felt. Along the inland waterways of North America, beaver skins became

(THE D'ORSAY.)
(1820)

FROM THE COLLECTIONS OF THE MUSEUM OF THE FUR TRADE, CHADRON, NEBRASKA

the coin of the times—and the beaver population in the east dwindled. Fierce competition broke out between the Hudson's Bay Company and its young rival, the North West Company, as they raced to extend trading lines west. Both commissioned explorers like Mackenzie to find cheaper transportation routes and new sources of furs. Left, voyageurs from the Bay Company load trading goods for an expedition into the interior. In the fall, the canoes would return with a valuable cargo of furs. Traders worked long hours in hazardous terrain, but some became well-to-do over the years.

"NAVY"
COCKED HAT.
(1800)

CLERICAL.
(Eighteenth Century)

(THE PARIS BEAU.)
(1815)

Riverbanks dissolve in a gleaming maze of ponds and channels: the Mackenzie River's 4,700-square-

mile delta. "We were much at a loss," noted Mackenzie, "what Channel out of some hundreds to take."

continent, fatigue and depression took their toll on Mackenzie. He suffered "much annoyance" from nightmares: "I could not close my eyes without finding myself in company with the Dead."

His mother had died when he was still a child, living on the Isle of Lewis in Scotland's Outer Hebrides. (The date of her death is lost; he was born in 1763 or 1764.) His father, Kenneth, decided to leave the impoverished island and seek a better life in British North America, taking his sisters and Alexander but leaving two small daughters with relatives in Scotland. Only a few months after the Mackenzies reached New York, fighting at Lexington and Concord flared into revolution; Kenneth Mackenzie joined a Loyalist regiment, and died in service in 1780.

Luckily, Alex had two aunts to care for him. They sent him to school in Montreal in 1778, and the next year he found work at the countinghouse of Finlay, Gregory & Co., fur traders.

Bloody antlers, freshly stripped of velvet, crown the bull barren-ground caribou in mid-September as rutting season approaches.

"Joining the fur trade was the romantic and adventurous thing for a young man to do," says Dr. W. Kaye Lamb, editor of Mackenzie's journals and letters. Formerly Dominion Archivist and National Librarian of Canada, he kindly shared his great knowledge of this period when I met him in Vancouver, British Columbia. As he points out, the little boy must have heard tales of the North back in Stornoway, where agents of the trade recruited able young men. After five years of office work, Mackenzie was ready to test himself in Indian country. His employer John Gregory, making him a partner in the firm, entrusted him with "a small adventure of goods" and he set out for Detroit in 1785.

Blond and strong and ambitious, he was entering a world of bitter rivalries beyond the difficulties of the wilderness. The high price of prime beaver pelts raised the stakes for all concerned. Although the peace

Known for their curiosity, caribou often stop to eye an intruder. Indians along Mackenzie's route wasted little of their kill, using sinews for snares or lines and antlers for club-like weapons.

treaty of 1783 gave Detroit to the United States, a British garrison held it for another 13 years; national tensions remained alive. Within Canada, rival firms vied with the old monopoly of the Hudson's Bay Company and with each other. By 1789 Mackenzie was a partner in the fast-expanding North West Company, authorized to find a new route across the continent to the Pacific Ocean—and the Orient.

He set out with a picked crew: four French-Canadian voyageurs, two of whom took their wives along, and a German whose presence is a mystery. Three Indians went as hunters and interpreters; their leader, called the English Chief, had learned the speech of the whites from the famous traveler Samuel Hearne of the Bay Company. The "chief" had two wives to himself.

Mackenzie's manuscript journal survives, a working account from 9 a.m. June 3, when the bark canoes left Fort Chipewyan on Lake Athabasca, till their return. Times of embarcation: "4 this Morning," "1/2 past 2 A.M.," or a rare late start after an issue of rum. Courses: "W. 21 Miles, then N.N.W. 9 miles. . . ." Dr. Lamb found that Mackenzie underestimated the distances he covered: he reckoned one day's travel at 69 miles when it was actually almost 80. Details of the route: "strong current," "landing is very steep." "The Portage is very bad and 535 paces long." "Men and Indians much fatigued." Notes on weather: "a strong N.N.E. wind all Day which hindered us much."

On June 9 they found Great Slave Lake covered with ice, but the hope of escaping "Muskettows and Gnatts" proved vain. Rain and wind plagued them till the ice broke up. I saw this immense lake at its most welcoming, on a beautiful autumn day, and the Mayor of Yellowknife took me out in his cabin cruiser to see the shoreline where Mackenzie camped. He and his party had to grope through channels cleared of ice by the wind, until they found the river they wanted on June 29.

Flock of ptarmigan races over snow-splotched tundra near the mouth of the Mackenzie. With body plumage brown in

STEPHEN J. KRASEMANN (ABOVE AND OPPOSITE)

Now they entered country not even their Indians had seen. They passed snowy mountains to the westward; they ran rapids, swatted mosquitoes, presented knives and blue beads to tribesmen they met. They left the woods behind them. By July 10 Mackenzie knew this river would lead him not to the Pacific but the "Northern Ocean." It splayed among islands: "We were much at a loss what Channel out of some hundreds to take."

I saw the Mackenzie Delta from the air, in a small plane. We flew low over a giant mosaic of shining, endless, intricate streams, a maze of ponds and islands and winding channels—as Mackenzie said, "very serpenting."

summer, ptarmigan turn white in winter. Frequent sightings of wildlife heartened the Mackenzie expedition as the landscape grew increasingly desolate above the Arctic Circle and near the ocean.

He wrote nothing about his frustration, but he may have been unable to hide it; his hard-bitten crew declared "themselves now and at any time ready to go with me wherever I choose to lead them," and they went on to the ocean his men were eager to see. On the foggy morning of July 14, a voyageur woke the others to see animals like "Pieces of Ice." Mackenzie knew they were whales, and pursued them in the canoe—"a very wild and unreflecting enterprise," he admitted.

Fortunately, whales and explorers escaped each other; and soon the humans turned homeward. "Weather disagreeably cold, Wind S.W.... We find the Current so strong here that we are obliged to Tow our Canoe with a line." Encounters—some civil, some tense—with Indians. Mackenzie rebuked the English Chief on a point of discipline, and calmed his fury with dinner and "a Dram or two." He settled the only quarrel in the crew. By September 12 they were safe at Fort Chipewyan.

Tradition, apt if not authentic, says he called his discovery the River Disappointment. Dissatisfied with his own ability to determine longitude and latitude, he spent the winter of 1791-1792 in London studying "the sciences of astronomy and navigation" and buying equipment. The next winter found him at an advance base on the Peace River, waiting to strike westward to the sea and, with luck, the great "River of the West"—the famous route now called the Columbia.

He had an able lieutenant, six voyageurs (two being veterans of the Arctic trip), two Indian interpreter-guides, a dog to help in hunting, and 3,000 pounds of supplies to fit into a 25-foot canoe. He also had the uneasy knowledge that a skilled surveyor from the Bay Company had been scouting the Athabasca country—his own firm might be outflanked in the west.

In May the rivers were free of ice, mosquitoes and sandflies active, grizzlies out of their dens. Mackenzie and his men set out up the Peace; on May 17 they sighted the Rockies. Soon the melt-swollen rapids of the Peace River Canyon forced them into the towing and portaging of a long, laborious struggle through unmapped mountains. They had escaped many natural dangers when, on June 13, they had 80 pounds of gunpowder spread out to dry. A crewman strolled across it "with a lighted pipe in his mouth.... one spark might have put a period to all my anxiety and ambition." Rumors of Indian treachery created panic on June 24, and the men wanted to turn back; the thought of "such a disappointment" caused Mackenzie "sensations little short of agony."

But within a month he was recording his success on a seaside rock, writing in vermilion and melted grease, and by early September he and his men were back at Fort Chipewyan—where he suffered through a winter of lassitude and horror.

"At least twice Mackenzie had something like a nervous breakdown," Dr. Lamb told me. "He was a somewhat unstable man—and a very proud man."

Risking their lives, Mackenzie and his men chase white whales through the ice-strewn waters of the Arctic Ocean. A flip of a tail could easily have spilled the bark canoe. Mackenzie's curiosity, which led to an occasional reckless venture, also spurred him to important feats of exploration.

Agleam with summer light, the Peace River snakes slowly through its noble valley. Mackenzie

marveled at this "magnificent theatre of nature" on his second "voyage of discovery."

Resources--
and
Perils

Dark bands of coal and shale stripe 150-foot cliffs near the head of Peace River Canyon. Falling rocks from cliffs above the river threatened Mackenzie's men as they

© J.A. KRAULIS / THE IMAGE BANK OF CANADA (ABOVE)

towed their canoe up the fierce rapids. Nearly swept away by the current, they escaped disaster by scaling the canyon wall and cutting a trail through the woods. Paper birch trees (above) supplied bark to repair the badly damaged canoe. In the midst of danger, Mackenzie noted the bounty of the wilderness— like these ripe raspberries growing in shaly soil.

I recalled an incident near the Pacific, when Indians threatened Mackenzie with daggers and he mentioned his reaction to the most hostile one: "my resentment predominated, and, if he had come within my reach, I verily believe, that I should have terminated his insolence for ever."

That wording, says Dr. Lamb, may owe something to "a very able hack writer, William Combe, who helped Mackenzie prepare his journals for publication." But the sentiment is certainly Mackenzie's; "he was not a man to drop a grievance."

Back in Montreal, he and young men like him would relax at the prestigious Beaver Club, limited at first to men who had spent at least one winter in the wilderness. They would start eating and drinking at four in the afternoon and go on until four in the morning. They could all drink with great skill. One night they danced on the tables until the plates and glasses and bottles were shattered and scattered over the assemblage. "After their time in the wild," Dr. Lamb remarks, "they naturally wanted to live it up. Mackenzie and his red-haired friend William McGillivray were especially noted for their wild parties."

It was McGillivray's formidable uncle, Simon McTavish of Montreal, whom Mackenzie challenged on an issue of continental scale: the policy of their now-powerful company. Mackenzie wanted to collect furs in the west and ship them from the Pacific coast direct to China. A romantic dream?

"He was a romantic, to some extent," says Dr. Lamb, "but this was a straightforward question of transportation costs."

McTavish, one of the richest merchant princes in Canada, balked. "He was a very imperious sort of man; he completely dominated the North West Company; and along comes Macken-

zie with different ideas—to divert trade from Montreal. That was McTavish's city, and it meant much to him."

Discussion, intrigue, quarrels—and inevitably McTavish won. A shareholder wrote: "as there could not be two Caesars in Rome one must remove." Mackenzie left the company "in a pet," furious, hot-headed, talking of revenge. He was in his mid-thirties, and his days of exploration were over.

He went to London, where he was knighted in 1802. He kept an interest in Canadian affairs, but after 1810 his home was in Britain. He enjoyed acclaim as an explorer; he had a comfortable amount of money; and he could afford to buy an estate in Scotland. He married "within the clan" in 1812, choosing teenaged Geddes Mackenzie, known for her beauty. He had left a natural son to make his own way in the northwest, but arranged for a natural daughter to be reared in Scotland. Lady Mackenzie bore him three children, but he did not see them grow up. Early in 1819 he wrote to his cousin and confidant, Roderic: "I have been overtaken with the consequences of my sufferings in the North West." He went to Edinburgh in January 1820 to seek medical help for what was probably Bright's disease; stricken on his way home, he died on March 12.

Today, place-names from the Arctic through British Columbia mark his routes and honor his memory, while a river that feeds the Fraser, and a lake in Ontario, commemorate the far-flung work of his obscure contemporary David Thompson.

Highly respected by his colleagues in his own time, Thompson had outlived most of them when he died, feeble and almost forgotten, late in his 86th year.

He was born in London of Welsh parents on April 30, 1770.

Mired in knee-deep mud, the Mackenzie party portages through swampy terrain between the Parsnip River and the McGregor. The waterlogged and battered canoe tested the strength of four men. Mackenzie ignored all such obstacles in his search for a navigable route.

His father died two years later, and in 1777 he entered a charity school called the Grey Coat Hospital. There he studied the math and geography needed by a navigator or surveyor, and amused himself with books like *Robinson Crusoe, Gulliver's Travels*, and tales of Sinbad the Sailor.

"David had a better education than most ship's captains of his time, much better than Charles Dickens," says Dr. Victor G. Hopwood of Vancouver. A specialist in Canadian literature, he is preparing a biography of Thompson. "When he left school, he was given a Hadley's quadrant and Robertson's *Elements of Navigation*, the most advanced treatise of the time."

He left in 1784, a "mathematical Boy" apprenticed to the Hudson's Bay Company for seven years' service in America. Another boy chosen for this work "eloped" in dismay, but David embarked in May and reached Fort Churchill in September. I can appreciate the courage it took for a youngster to make his way in that desolate country after visiting Churchill on a dreary, cold, and foggy day in autumn. Around the landing field today, a few abandoned buildings cluster in a hulking snowy expanse of wilderness. From the beginning David was alert to this strange new life: the polar bear that "swims with ease and swiftness," the winter cold "so intense that everything in a manner is shivered by it."

Setting sun bronzes the cloud-draped waters of Dean Channel, west of Mackenzie Rock. Threatened by hostile Indians, Mackenzie took refuge on an outcrop of rock (foreground). Despite the pleas of his men, he refused to leave until he painted his famous inscription, now restored. The remote spot—westernmost point of his journey— marks his arrival at the Pacific Coast.

His account of summer's mosquitoes reveals his informality and humor: "Smoke is no relief, they can stand more smoke than we can, and smoke cannot be carried about with us . . . they are a terrour to every creature on dry lands if swamps may be so called. . . . A sailor finding swearing of no use, tried what Tar could do, and covered his face with it, but the musketoes stuck to it in such numbers as to blind him, and the tickling of their wings was worse than their bites. . . ."

At first he worked as a clerk. Then, on duty inland, he fell down a riverbank and broke his right leg. While it mended, the company's able surveyor Philip Turnor taught him the "practical astronomy" he could use in the field. He lost the sight of his right eye doing calculations by candlelight, but he gained a new career as explorer, surveyor, and mapmaker. With a gimpy leg and a blind eye, he would travel 50,000 miles through the northwest—afoot, on horseback, or by canoe.

I could not hope to retrace so many journeys, so I was especially interested in the opinion of a man who did: J. B. Tyrrell of the Geological Survey of Canada, who traveled many of the same routes between 1883 and 1898, checking Thompson's observations by his own. Conceding that "my instruments may have been

better," Tyrrell found Thompson's accuracy so astonishing that he prepared a pioneer edition of his writings. One scholar had called Thompson "the greatest geographer of his day in British America"; Tyrrell thought him "the greatest practical land geographer that the world has produced."

His apprenticeship completed in 1791, Thompson accepted a contract with the company for £15 a year. He soon became involved in its efforts to secure the trade of the Athabasca country and edge out the "Montrealers." By 1796 his employers planned to make him "Master to the Northward"—that is, field manager at age 26 for as vast a field as he could conquer. But he left them when his contract expired and joined the North Westers as a surveyor.

Dr. Richard Glover, who has edited his work and whom I met at his home in Ottawa, takes a critical view. He points out that Thompson had not given the year's notice required by his contract. Moreover, he says, "One doubts that Thompson would have done well as 'Master.'" The aggressive leadership of Alexander Mackenzie was not Thompson's way.

For his new employers he carried out the work that stirred Mackenzie's praise. One episode from 1796 shows how narrow the margin of safety could be. Thompson was scouting Black River with two young Indians. Their inexperience with a tow line sent him riding the canoe down a 12-foot fall. Losing all their gunpowder and half their clothes, they nearly starved. They caught two fledgling eagles, but the fat caused a "violent" dysentery. Then they met some Indians who could supply food, ammunition, and shoes, and they went on with "cheerful hearts."

In June 1799, at Île-à-la-Crosse Lake, Thompson married 14-year-old Charlotte Small, daughter of an Indian mother and a fur trader. She shared some of his travels, bearing five children at remote posts in the west and eight more in eastern Canada after 1812. He taught her to read and write, and no doubt their devotion deepened his understanding of Indian life. By 1799 this was already extensive.

Thompson told, for example, how a fur trader panicked and scrambled up the tent poles when a polar bear invaded the tent. Another trader fought the bear with a musket while an

White and dangerous the year round, a polar bear rambles through high grass near Hudson Bay. Coming to this region of British North America as a 14-year-old apprentice in the fur trade, David Thompson thrived on the excitement and rigors of wilderness life. Between the years 1784 and 1812, he traveled 50,000 miles as he explored and surveyed the far northwest.

Indian woman rained blows on its head with an ax. When the bear died growling, she threatened to brain the coward if he came down. As Thompson explained, "the Indian woman pardons man for everything but want of courage; this is her sole support and protection...."

Thompson did not ignore the tragedies of the wilderness, such as the winter famine when parents might be driven to feed their stronger children with the body of the youngest. He saw how the fortunate appearance of game might strengthen faith in the pity of the Manito, the ruling Spirit.

A devout Christian himself, he studied Indian beliefs with care, consulting old men and sharing significant moments. As he recorded of some Nahathaways: "After a weary day's march we sat by a log fire... with thousands of sparkling stars passing before us, we could not help enquiring who lived in those bright mansions; for I frequently conversed with them as one of themselves." He explained the brilliant planets, and his companions decided they were "abodes of the spirits of those who had led a good life." He could make a spirit of the dark pine forest as vivid as his own memory of the devil: "Pah kok, a tall hateful spirit... his howlings are heard in the storm, he delights to add to its terrors... when he approaches a Tent and howls, he announces the death of one of the inmates; of all beings he is the... most dreaded."

The authorities on Thompson's life agree in praise of his style. Dr. Lamb calls him "the most colorful and readable" of all the fur-trade authors. Dr. Glover calls him "a master storyteller" and points out that nobody else in his time had seen so much of the country, known so much of its most significant trade, and could give so interesting an account.

"I was attracted to him first of all because he could write so well," Dr. Hopwood told me as we sat in his study—he had just built some extra bookcases to house his own large library. "The historical interest was there, of course, but the writing drove me on to learn more of Thompson's character."

In assessing his character, they disagree, especially with regard to his last years in the far west, from 1807 to 1813. Beyond the vague limits of the Louisiana Purchase lay the rich Oregon

Berry plants in autumn near Fort Churchill disclose key differences to the close observer.

Bearberry (left) and crowberry (right) flank cranberry, with its small, waxy leaves. A self-taught naturalist, Thompson described the berries in his detailed— and often poetic—field journals. "For the age of guessing is passed away," he explained, "and the traveller is expected to give his reasons for what he asserts."

country, open to trade but already subject to conflicting claims. Lewis and Clark's winter in the lower Columbia Valley—1805-1806—lent color to a claim by the United States. In the spring of 1807 Thompson began trading and exploring in the region, and by July 1811 he was posting a claim for Great Britain and "the N. W. Company of Merchants from Canada." When he wrote this paper and tied it to a small pole, he was just half a mile from the point where the Snake River joins the Columbia.

Had the company ordered him into a race against an American party? Was he supposed to be making all speed downriver and establishing a post at its mouth before John Jacob Astor's men from New York could get there by sea around Cape Horn?

No written orders survive. Thompson himself left conflicting statements. In an undated private memorandum, he wrote that he was "obliged to take 4 canoes and . . . oppose" Astor's men. When he reached his destination on July 15, he found "four low Log Huts, the far famed Fort Astoria of the United States," and then he gave the Americans' leaders a letter. This stated that the North West partners had accepted Astor's offer of a one-third share in the venture.

If Thompson expected to meet new colleagues, he had no special reason to hurry. His admirers think this was the case. If sent to forestall rivals, he failed. His critics think he did, when a bolder man would have succeeded. In any case, the deal with Astor was never completed.

After a courteous welcome at Astoria, Thompson finished his exploration of the Columbia. He was not only the first white man to trace the length of the river, but also the geographer who mapped its perplexing northeastern tributaries. He had com-

Thompson in peril on the Black River fights to straighten his canoe at a 12-foot fall. He and the two Indians—whose inexperience caused the emergency—had stowed pants and shoes as they towed the canoe. All three escaped serious injury in the mishap— with little left to wear, no food, no ammunition.

piled his usual notes on terrain and trees and insects, Indian actions, customs, and food. And he had found a route via Athabasca Pass that would serve the fur trade for half a century.

By this route he made his way east to Fort William, on Lake Superior, for the annual summer meeting of company partners and a reunion with his family. Then, in July 1812, a ship brought news of war—with the United States. With all haste the season's collection of furs was packed, and the family joined the rush to safety in Montreal. Thompson at 42 had seen the western wilderness for the last time.

He expected to leave it anyway. His bad leg bothered him, he was "getting tired of such constant hard journeys," and he wanted his boys and girls to have "an equal and good education."

During the war he worked on his maps, which others quarried for years without giving him credit. After it, he was appointed as astronomer to the British commission to establish the boundary with the United States, from near Montreal west to Lake of the Woods. He worked at this from 1816 till 1826. When his American counterpart resigned, the Americans didn't replace him—they accepted the observations of "Mr. Astronomer Thompson" as accurate and binding on both powers. As Dr. Hopwood says, "a tribute to his integrity!"

No likeness of Thompson has survived, but Dr. John J. Bigsby of the British commission described him as "short and compact" of figure, quiet of manner and plainly dressed, with an odd "cut-short" snub nose and a Welsh accent. Bigsby, a shrewd and cultivated man, noticed how he would read Scripture to the voyageurs in French "most extraordinarily pronounced," or explain their mission to an Indian: "to find how far north the shadow of the United States extended, and how far south the shadow of their great father, King George."

The survey over, Thompson returned to the farm he had bought at Williamstown in Upper Canada (now Ontario). He tried in vain to persuade British officials to press a claim to the Oregon country. He had retired from the fur trade a prosperous man, but his affairs went badly. He could not finish his maps to his own satisfaction, or sell them at a fair price. He was generous—he once bought the instruments of a bankrupt colleague for a handsome price—and he found it painful to collect debts from neighbors. He had invested in a store; when a depression overtook the region, the store failed. He went back to local surveying to scrape up an income. He pawned his overcoat, his surveyor's level, his theodolite, his cherished sextant.

"He suffered bad health," says Dr. Hopwood, "when he needed good health most." He labored over his notes, hoping that an account of his travels would interest a publisher, and then he lost the sight of his good eye.

Tradition pictured him as dying blind, in abject poverty, but Dr. Hopwood found that in 1848 a surgeon was able to restore

Summer: Between the Snows

Crystal drop on a blade of grass reflects the shore of Turtle Lake in northern Minnesota. In 1798 Thompson traced the Mississippi to this remote lake: Later surveys show nearby Lake Itasca as the source. "Everywhere there was much wild rice," he wrote, "upon which the wild fowl fed...." In August, an immature mallard washes its wings; other waterfowl feed among brome-grass full with seed (upper right). Stirred by the riches

STEPHEN J. KRASEMANN (ABOVE)

of the region, Thompson predicted: "Whatever the Nile has been in ancient times in arts and arms, the noble valley of the Mississippi bids fair to be...."

Misting in sub-zero cold, the almost-frozen Bow River bends southeast beneath the craggy citadel of Mount Eisenhower. Fur traders like Thompson heard of this route, but the Piegan Indians kept

them away with threats because they wanted to prevent their foes the Kutenais from obtaining firearms. Sternly warned off by the Piegans, Thompson found alternative ways to the west.

the vision of both eyes. Thompson told the doctor happily one morning that he had seen a star his bad eye had last seen when he was 19 years old. After reaching 80 he gave up trying to write; but he could still enjoy reading, and he lived on in his daughters' care until 1857. A grandson paid for the graveyard plot, where Charlotte was buried beside him three months later; and J. B. Tyrrell, who brought his *Travels* to a belated publication, paid for a gravestone in 1927.

"Thompson was a very independent man," Dr. Hopwood says in summary. "He wouldn't give in, even to old age. He struggled as long as he could."

In this, Thompson resembles that very different man Mackenzie. Moreover, both were resourceful; they had to be, in the wilderness. Once, on Mackenzie's Pacific journey, Indians helped themselves to some unguarded utensils. He could not spare these items and could hardly afford a quarrel, so he blamed the villagers' relatives "who were gone." Then he gravely informed his audience that white men controlled the ocean: If his goods were not returned, no salmon would be permitted to come upriver. In short, "we possessed the power to starve them and their children. . . . This finesse succeeded." Everything was brought back. "We purchased several large salmon . . . and enjoyed the delicious meal which they afforded."

Thompson saw from the first that the "vile" rum and brandy of the traders were degrading native life. Once, ordered to carry two kegs of liquor to the Indians, he obeyed: ". . . when we came to the defiles of the Mountains, I placed the two Kegs of Alcohol

Water routes of Thompson's journeys vein the continent from Hudson Bay to the Pacific. Patient explorer and careful mapmaker, he emphasized details as much as discovery. His major accomplishments: exploring the full 1,200 miles of the Columbia River and opening the Athabasca Pass, a major route of the fur trade.

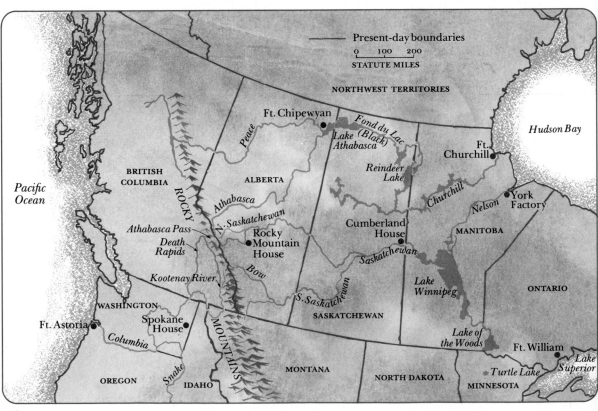

on a vicious horse; and by noon the Kegs were empty, and in pieces, the Horse rubbing his load against the Rocks to get rid of it. . . ." He warned his partners that he would do the same to any other keg. This ruse disposed of "the sad sight of drunkenness" within his area of responsibility for six years.

I recalled this episode in Yellowknife, a gold-mining town with the new amenities and the old toughness. I saw three men, two Indians and one white, bodily ejected from a bar. It was pay-day; some men, like the roisterers of the Beaver Club, would celebrate with a spree.

Near Inuvik, in the farthest northwestern area of the Northwest Territories, I saw the oil rigs in the serpentine waters of the Mackenzie Delta. More rigs are at work offshore, in the shallows of the Beaufort Sea. I talked with the bearded men of the energy industry, and wondered if a modern Mackenzie would join them and make a career of it. He had a vision of trade on a giant scale; he had insight, and drive—but Dr. Glover suspects he would have been "too quarrelsome" to have been a good business partner for anyone very long.

In Inuvik proper, I walked along Mackenzie Road, a single mud street, scheduled for paving, that serves the "business district." The principal shop is still that of the Hudson's Bay Company. About half the residents are white; the rest, Inuit and Indian. They see TV programs from the Canadian Broadcasting Corporation, via satellite: David Thompson, I decided, would collect some fine anecdotes about that. I attended a service at the famous "igloo church," the white-domed church of Our Lady of Victory. Thompson would have been interested in this, too.

He sketched a vivid portrayal of the Inuit hunter—"Esquimaux": "naturally industrious, very ingenious, fond of the comforts of life so far as they can attain them, always cheerful, and even gay; it is true that in the morning, when he is about to embark in his shell of a Canoe, to face the waves of the sea, and the powerful animals he has to contend with, for food and clothing for himself and family, he is for many minutes very serious, because he is a man of reflection, knows the dangers to which he is exposed, but steps into his canoe, and bravely goes through the toil and dangers of the day."

The great explorers did as much; many details evoke their lives today.

Only the land itself reveals the scale of their achievement.

It was a gorgeous fall afternoon when I saw the Mackenzie Delta from the air, flying for hours over shining lakes and winding tapestries of streams until I was awed by the ability of men to venture among them with no maps, no shelter, no chance of rescue by air or sea or land. I was daunted by the immensity of that airscape.

By fur-trade standards, of course, I never suffered at all as I tried to recapture a past beyond frontiers. I did tramp through

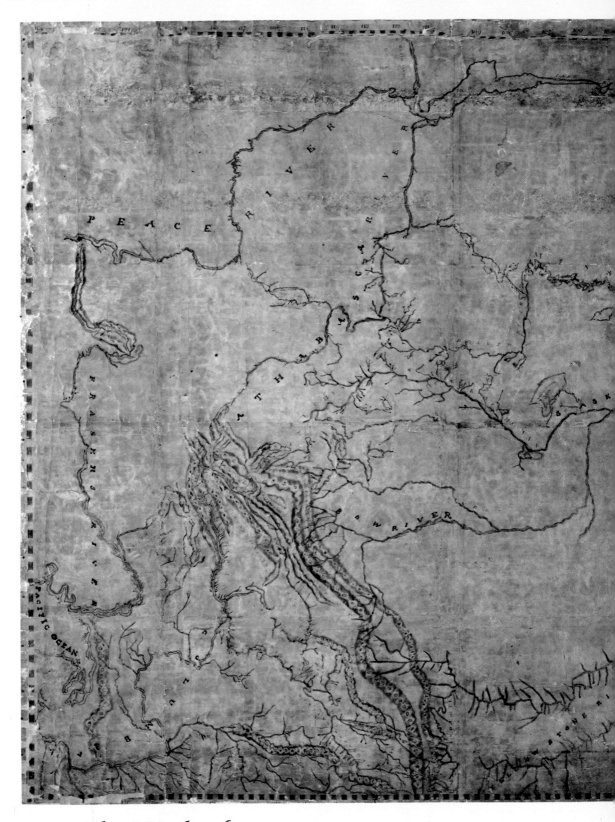

The Work of 20 Years

Thompson's masterpiece—a map 6'5" x 10'—still startles observers with its accuracy. "I have fully completed the survey of this part of North America from sea to sea . . . ," Thompson stated in 1811. A

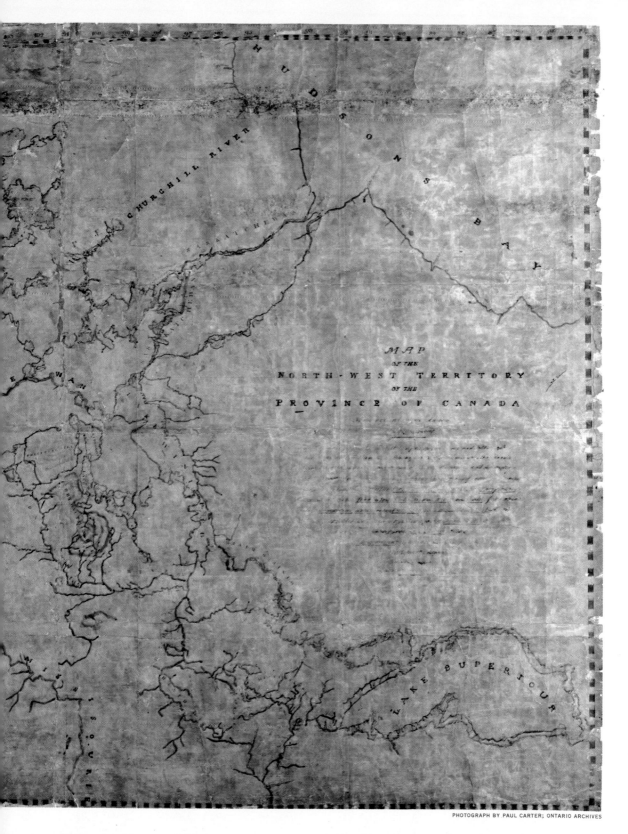

MAP

OF THE

NORTH-WEST TERRITORY

OF THE

PROVINCE OF CANADA

son sold it to the Ontario government about 1857; officials consulted but did not publish it. Although a prime source for future maps, it failed to gain Thompson the recognition he deserved.

Overleaf: Sighting his sextant on an artificial horizon, Thompson determines the latitude of Death Rapids. Thus he mapped the full length of the Columbia.

the woods on occasion—and slap at insects—and feel disgust at the softness that city living had created. I marveled again and again at the miles and the speed that Mackenzie and Thompson and their men could get out of a given day, on foot or on horseback or on the water. I saw them crashing through undergrowth or scrambling over muskeg or running rapids, sleeping on the ground for a few hours and starting again the next day. Starting sometimes grimly, more often with high morale and a sense of mission.

One lovely day I lingered by a picnic table at Rocky Mountain House in southwestern Alberta. This was the base for many of Thompson's journeys, his home for three winters. Here the North Saskatchewan River swings on a wide bend through spacious prairie. Mist rose gently above the gleaming water past the dark conifers. Before many weeks the stream would freeze to a dull sheen of an ax blade.

In his later years he would long for this country: "give me a gallop into the natural meadows, the glorious hunting-grounds ... with their clear skies and bracing airs.... Let me listen at the close of the day to the cries of the wild creatures, as I sit at the door of my skin-tent—to the loud whistle of the stag, the sullen, gong-like boom of the elk, the bellow of the bison, or the wolf-howl."

Survival in the wilderness depends on many things, not least on understanding among men. In winter camp near the Bow River, an old Indian gave Thompson a warning: "If one of our people offers you his left hand, give him your left hand, for the right hand is no mark of friendship. This hand wields the spear, draws the Bow and the trigger of the gun; it is the hand of death. The left hand is next to the heart and speaks truth and friendship; it holds the shield of protection and is the hand of life."

I think I came closest to clasping that hand in Mackenzie's country, on a wide reach of a river in British Columbia. A friend and I were traveling by canoe, the water powerful and rushing but the surface unbroken except by our paddles. The bright sun of October had begun to spill lengthening shadows across the rolling terrain. A radio gave a light background of music as we entered a remarkably beautiful bend; we exchanged brief remarks on the timelessness of the place. The music changed; a local station was bringing us Indian chants, authentic music recorded nearby, men's deep voices in haunting, melodic cadences. The shiver we felt was the joy of recognition.

Dominance at stake, bighorn rams battle during rutting season in the Bow Valley. At right, bald eagles take waterside perches during the annual salmon run in Glacier

National Park. Thompson once remarked, "the eagle never loses his courage...." Displaying a similar resolve, Thompson claimed a vast new region for the British Crown.

Autumn storm clouds gather over the Columbia River, final leg of an epic

5   Lewis and Clark:

western expedition captained by Lewis and Clark between 1804 and 1806.

the Corps of Discovery BY RON FISHER

F rancis Scott Key was scribbling spare-time verses. Robert Fulton was in France, tinkering with his new steamboat. Napoleon was collecting barges for an invasion of England, and Lord Nelson was directing countermeasures at sea. Beethoven was struggling with another symphony—his third—and Goya was turning out one incisive portrait after another.

And at St. Charles, a muddy village on the Missouri River a few miles above St. Louis, a band of "robust helthy hardy young men" was just setting off on a voyage of discovery. Their mission: to ascend the Missouri to its source, make as easy a portage as possible, and descend the Columbia River to the Pacific Ocean.

It was 1804 and, through luck and adroit diplomacy, President Thomas Jefferson had lately acquired the vast territory of Louisiana from Napoleon. With a stroke of the pen and 15 million dollars, he doubled the area of the United States and added resources impossible to calculate. Jefferson had been curious about the Louisiana country for years, had wondered what treasures might lie hidden in its mysterious interior. He had gathered in his library all the available accounts from Britain and France as well as from Indians and trappers, trying to piece together a solution to the greatest mystery of all: Did a Northwest Passage indeed exist? Was there—as geographers and explorers had for centuries insisted there must be—a water route through the continent, a practical trade route to the riches of the Orient?

By careful study of the best sources he could find, Jefferson had acquired a wildly misleading impression. Long before anyone but Indians had seen the Rocky Mountains, as early as the 1720's, European mapmakers were drawing a range of mountains in the west, a minor feature rather like the Blue Ridge. Later versions added new discoveries, balancing the headwaters of the Missouri on the east and the headwaters of the Columbia on the west. Jefferson's best maps showed the "Stony Mountains" as a single narrow chain: An easy portage separated the two great river systems.

Reading Mackenzie's account of his struggle to the Pacific, Jefferson singled out one point of detail, the short portage between inland and Pacific slope drainage. It strengthened the optimistic view of a comfortable way to the South Sea—a one-day walk between rivers, or perhaps half a day.

So Jefferson launched his "Corps of Discovery"—an expedition he had been actively planning since 1801—and named as its leader his secretary Meriwether Lewis, who chose as his co-captain a friend of Army days, William Clark. Both were accomplished woodsmen, men of distinguished intelligence and superb common sense. They recruited a small group of men—about 30 would finally make the trip—and spent the winter of 1803-1804

Capt. William Clark, USA, outranked his future partner when they met on duty. Picked by Lewis as co-captain in 1803, he proved an accomplished mapmaker as well as an adroit negotiator with Indians. Later a governor of the Missouri Territory, he died in St. Louis in 1838.

encamped across the Mississippi from the mouth of the Missouri, molding their corps of volunteers into a disciplined Army unit. In the spring they finished outfitting. Into a keelboat they packed 21 bales of presents for Indians—not quite enough, it would turn out—14 bags of cornmeal, 15 barrels of flour, 7 barrels of salt—again, not enough—50 kegs of pork, 50 bushels of meal, tools, and medical supplies. These included "1. Tourniquet," "3. Best Lancets," "4 oz. Laudanum," and "50 doz. Bilious Pills."

They had three boats, a 55-foot keelboat that carried a squaresail and 22 oars, and two pirogues, canoe-like open boats.

On Monday, May 21, 1804, at St. Charles, the party was united, packed up, confident, and anxious to go: "Set out at half passed three oClock under three Cheers from the gentlemen on the bank," wrote Clark.

Their journey—a two-year epic—would accomplish important geographic and political goals. It would also produce the splendid *Journals* of the expedition. According to their editor Bernard DeVoto, they are "by far the most interesting as well as the most important original narrative of North American exploration."

I first encountered the *Journals* about ten years ago. Since then I've dipped into them frequently and with pleasure. They provide wonderful vicarious thrills to an armchair explorer. Some incidents never lose their appeal: the awful traverse of the Bitterroot Mountains, the misery of the lower Columbia, the relief when finally the ocean is in view. And my respect for the authors has been rising ever since the first morning I tried to cook breakfast for myself in the woods.

Both captains kept a record, and to read it is to accompany two articulate, curious, self-confident men through adventures that are exciting, funny, exhilarating, and humbling. Confrontations with Indians, grizzly bears, rapids, and backbreaking toil are handled with aplomb. "Sergeant Pryor in takeing down the mast put his Sholder out of Place, we made four trials before we replaced it." Hardy sergeant!

Lewis and Clark shared command on an equal basis, and if they disagreed or argued once during the 28 months of the trip the *Journals* do not record it. Lewis was the more introverted, often walking along the shore with his Newfoundland dog, Scannon. Clark was the engineer and geographer and the better boatman—and one of the world's worst, but most delightful, spellers: "Muskeetors verry troublesom," he wrote. Again, "passed much falling timber apparently the ravages of a Dreddfull harican." He referred to a conference with Indians "ounder a orning."

It took the Corps two and a half months to reach the vicinity of Council Bluffs, a name they gave the area after a meeting with

Meriwether Lewis, a veteran of frontier service, became Thomas Jefferson's secretary in 1801. The President soon chose the introspective young Virginian to lead a Corps of Discovery to the Pacific Ocean. Lewis died mysteriously in 1809, apparently a suicide.

some Oto and Missouri Indians. Clark thought it a "verry proper place for a Tradeing establishment." Much of the journey thus far had been difficult—the "muskeetors" remained troublesome, and it was often necessary to tow the boats against the current. But game was plentiful, and much of the trip sounds like fun. Clark noted: "Cat fish is cought in any part of the river. Turkeys Geese & a Beaver Killed & Cought every thing in prime order men in high Spirits. a fair Still evening. . . ."

On August 20, Sergeant Charles Floyd died—incredibly, the only casualty the party would suffer. He probably died of a ruptured appendix, an ailment that, in those days, would have killed him in New York or Boston. The men elected Patrick Gass to his position. They "proceeded on."

Other misadventures were minor by comparison. Snags, sandbars, driftwood, and squalls could be expected but not predicted. A few disciplinary problems among the men were taken care of—either by dismissal or by flogging, a punishment that horrified the Indians.

A show of force and some tense diplomacy saw the party through one awkward encounter with a band of truculent Teton Sioux. The Sioux habitually exacted tribute from fur traders, a sort of toll, and demanded as much from the Corps. Lewis and Clark offered presents but refused payment, and displayed their ordnance: which included a small cannon and two blunderbusses mounted on swivels. In the end neither arrows nor rifles were fired, and the Corps had no more trouble with Indians until they reached coastal tribes corrupted by contact with whites.

They spent the winter near present-day Bismarck, North Dakota, among the Mandan Indians, a people still secure in their own ways. Mandan hospitality—marked in David Thompson's words by "an almost total want of chastity"—had won this tribe friends in the fur trade; Clark stressed their desire to "be at peace with all nations."

As I found on a January visit, winter can be brutal in North Dakota. Snow lies thick and crusted in the silent woods. The only sounds are the wind, whistling in the bare branches, the crunch of your footsteps, the heave and hiss of your breath as you plod through the snow. The Missouri, locked tight, is rumpled and dimpled with bulges from the earlier ice of autumn. Unending wisps of snow blow across it, like rushing mountain streams.

The Corps of Discovery built themselves a stockade, Fort Mandan, and settled in for the long season. The captains occupied themselves with an interim report to President Jefferson. The report, along with Indian artifacts and zoological and botanical specimens, would be sent back to St. Louis in the spring.

One day they were joined by a French-Canadian trapper and fur trader, Toussaint Charbonneau. One of his wives, an Indian girl named Sacagawea, would become nearly as famous as Lewis and Clark. She was a Shoshoni, it turned out, abducted from her people several years before. She could be useful when the Corps

Distinctive regalia marks Pehriska-Ruhpa as a warrior of highest rank in the Dog Band, a society of honor in the Hidatsa tribe. He wears its headdress of magpie, raven, and eagle feathers, with a war whistle hung from his neck. His right hand

grips his schischikué, a charmed rattle. Artist Karl Bodmer painted the portrait in 1834, during a stay at Fort Clark on the Missouri. Across the river some 30 years earlier, Lewis and Clark had wintered among the Mandan Indians. To one of the chiefs they gave Jefferson's peace medal, a symbol of friendship presented to Indians throughout the West.

Times of Ordeal
in Mandan Country

Excruciating self-torture, self-imposed, proves the fortitude of Mandan braves in the four-day ritual called Okipa. They dangle from skewers piercing their breasts or shoulders. "... attendants hung upon the other skewers the young man's shield, bow and quiver, etc.," wrote artist George Catlin, the first white man to record the rite, "and in many instances the heavy skull of a buffalo. . . ." Other agonies followed. The bravest of all would have one or two fingers lopped off, then be dragged by runners around a large cylindrical altar (below) that held sacred relics. About 1700, some 8,000 Mandans lived around present-day Bismarck, North Dakota. In the 1780's smallpox struck, weakening them and forcing them northward away from the more warlike Sioux—where Lewis and Clark found them. Catlin produced portraits of several, including 12-year-old Sha-ko-ka with the gray hair rather common in the tribe; Seehk-hee-da, a noted brave; and an aged chief happy to recall the visit of "Red Hair" (Clark) and "Long Knife" (Lewis) 28 years earlier. That winter had brought the captains varied, prolonged worries. Frostbite plagued the hunters, and the boats froze in the river, where the ice nearly destroyed them.

entered the land of the Shoshoni somewhere near the Rocky Mountains. And Charbonneau spoke the difficult tongue of the Minnetaree, who lived upriver. So the decision was made: Charbonneau and Sacagawea would come along. On February 11 Sacagawea bore her first child, so the party now included not only a black slave—Clark's strong and resourceful servant York—a dog, and a woman, but also a papoose.

Hunting, smoking meat, gathering firewood, and other chores kept the men busy during the slow harsh winter. On December 17 "about 8 oClock P M. the thermometer fell to 74° below the freesing pointe." In January, "a Cold Day Thermometer at 21° below 0 . . . Several Indians Call at the Fort nearly frosed."

When spring finally came, the captains sent the keelboat back to St. Louis and set off in the two pirogues and six canoes that the men had made during the winter. Their boats were "not quite so rispectable as those of Columbus or Capt. Cook," Lewis wrote, but "still viewed by us with as much pleasure as those deservedly famed adventurers ever beheld theirs."

As he soberly added, "we were now about to penetrate a country at least two thousand miles in width, on which the foot of civilized man had never trodden; the good or evil it had in store for us was for experiment yet to determine. . . ."

Both good and evil awaited them, far into the wilderness and across the unknown mountains.

The longest sustained camping trip I ever made—on a river in Alaska—lasted about a month, and during that month I got heartily tired of the routine of camping: the little daily chores that go into keeping yourself fed, sheltered, warm, and dry, to say nothing of traveling a certain number of miles every day. Day after day we set up camp every evening and tore it down again every morning. Food had to be prepared every day, rain or shine. And the dishes washed.

The Lewis and Clark *Journals* don't dwell on day-to-day routine, except to record what the hunters brought in, but the secondary work of traveling about 18 miles a day must have been trying. Now I reread with greater admiration such entries as this: "all the party in high Sperits they pass but fiew nights without amuseing themselves danceing possessing perfect harmony and good understanding towards each other. . . ."

As they proceeded upriver from Fort Mandan, game became more and more plentiful. "Emence" herds of bison, deer and elk, with bear and beaver, kept the party well fed. One day, Lewis wrote, "The party killed two Elk and Buffaloe today, and my dog caught a goat, which he overtook by superior fleetness, the goat it must be understood was with young and extreemly poor."

They began to encounter grizzly bears, an animal they had been warned about but whose ferocity they had doubted. Lewis felt confident they could dispatch any bear with ease: "the Indians may well fear this anamal . . . with their bows and arrows . . . but in the hands of skillfull riflemen, they are by no means as formidable or dangerous as they have been represented."

Further encounters would shake his confidence. On May 5, Clark and one of the hunters killed a grizzly, but only after firing ten rifle balls into him—five through his lungs. They measured his "tallons" at 4 3/8 inches long. "I find that the curiossity of our party is pretty well satisfyed with rispect to this anamal."

A few days later, six "good hunters" attacked a grizzly that even with a shoulder broken chased two of his attackers into the river and almost got one of them before a brain shot killed him.

That same day—a hard day!—one of the pirogues suffered near disaster. With Charbonneau at the helm, a sudden squall turned the boat onto her side, and she would have gone "com-

Wheeling from a buffalo he has shot, Lewis faces a stalking grizzly. His weapons: an empty rifle and an espontoon, the lightweight pike that had become a mark of rank for an officer, useful as a walking stick. The bear "pitched at me, open mouthed and full speed," Lewis

pletely topsaturva" without the "resistance" of an awning against the water. Charbonneau, "perhaps the most timid waterman in the world," was "crying to his god for mercy." Cruzatte, the bowman, had to threaten "to shoot him instantly" to make him "take hold of the rudder and do his duty." Sacagawea, also in this boat with her baby, remained calm, plucking from the water most of the lightweight supplies that washed overboard.

By late May they were deep in the wilderness, in country about which they had little information except what they had gleaned from Indians. The terrain was changing—no more the garden-like Great Plains. "This is truly a desert barren country," Lewis wrote as the Corps crossed what is now central Montana. Progress up the increasingly rapid and shallow Missouri became more difficult. At riffles and rocky places the men spent a fourth

wrote. "I ran haistily into the water...." He turned "and presented the point of my espontoon" as the bear came "within about 20 feet." Luckily the bear veered and fled "as if frightened." Earlier Lewis had written that he would rather fight "two Indians than one bear."

of their time in cold water "even to their armpits." Tenacious mud on banks and bluffs forced them to work barefoot, "draging the heavy burthen of a canoe" over patches of "sharp fragments of rocks . . . in short their labour is incredibly painfull and great, yet those faithfull fellows bear it without a murmur."

Most of the Missouri River would be unrecognizable to them today. Dams have slowed and tamed the mighty river, flooding the riffles and rapids that the "faithfull fellows" struggled against. But I have seen one section, below Great Falls, Montana, that is essentially unchanged—and spectacular. Here erosion has sculpted the white cliffs to what Lewis called "a most romantic appearance." It inspired one of the most famous passages of the *Journals*, his description of scenes of "visionary inchantment."

Instinctive geographers of great skill, Lewis and Clark faced a puzzle at the mouth of the Marias River, a river they had not expected to encounter: Neither their maps nor their Indian informants had mentioned it. Which fork was the main stream of the Missouri? As Lewis knew, "to mistake the stream [now] . . . and to ascend such stream to the rocky Mountain or perhaps much further . . . and then be obliged to return and take the other stream would not only loose us the whole of this season but would probably so dishearten the party that it might defeat the expedition altogether."

Within a few hours both Lewis and Clark had settled in their own minds which fork was the true Missouri—the south branch—but the rest of the Corps, to a man, disagreed with them. So they stopped at the confluence for a few days while small parties explored a few miles up each river. The captains were proved right when Lewis, reconnoitering ahead, recognized a "tremendious" roaring as the sound of "the great falls of the Missouri," a landmark famous among the Indians. The majesty of the falls—five cataracts within ten miles—astounded Lewis, one *"pleasingly beautifull,"* another *"sublimely grand."* Sublime, perhaps, but here, "hising flashing and sparkling" in their path, was one of the greatest obstacles they would face.

The portage stretched 18 miles across hot acres of prickly-pear cactus whose spines pierced the men's moccasins. They devised a sort of wagon—cutting up a pirogue mast for axles—and heaved and tugged at the heavy cargo. Clark wrote that "the men has to haul with all their strength wate & art . . . maney limping from the soreness of their feet

(Continued on page 141)

"From the reflection of the sun on the sprey or mist which arrises from these falls," wrote Lewis in June 1805, "is a beautifull rainbow produced. . . ." Rainbow Falls survives as a cascade today though power dams have altered most of the ten-

JEFF FOOTT

mile-long Great Falls. Lewis and Clark spent two weeks portaging around them, slowed by heat, storms, cactus— and backbreaking labor. But they feasted on buffalo meat. Of the coyote, then unknown to science, Lewis wrote that it "barks like a dog, they frequently salute us with this note as we pass through the plains."

DICK DURRANCE II (OPPOSITE)

Animals of the Great Plains

One ton of dusty fury charges across the National Bison Range in Montana. Herds of buffalo—incredibly placid— kept the Corps well fed. "I passed several [buffalo] . . . within fifty paces," Lewis wrote; "they viewed me for a moment as something novel and then very unconcernedly continued to feed." Lewis and Clark saw approximately 175 new species or subspecies of plants, more than 100 of

animals, including the prairie rattlesnake and the prairie dog. The snakes kept the explorers wary: Lewis once awoke to find one coiled just ten feet away. Prairie dogs intrigued the men. Clark noted that one village covered "about 4 acres of Ground" and contained innumerable burrows. At their mouths the little animals would sit erect, "make a Whistleing noise and whin allarmed Step into their hole."

Clouds brush the peaks of the Bitterroot Range on the Idaho-Montana border. Racing the

onset of winter, the Corps struggled 11 days to cross this unexpectedly formidable barrier.

some become fant for a fiew moments, but no man complains all go chearfully on." Their troubles were only beginning, and they knew it: "We all believe that we are about to enter on the most perilous and dificuelt part of our Voyage," noted Clark. By June 20 they could see snow glitter on mountains to the north and west. Here, on the maps, would be a single ridge, the mirror image of the Appalachians. . . . Here, in reality, were the massive ranges of the Rockies: "one rang above another as they receede from the river . . . the adjacent mountains commonly rise so high as to conceal the more distant . . . from our view."

The Three Forks of the Missouri repeated the riddle of the Marias, with greater urgency. They named the three rivers—the Gallatin, the Madison, the Jefferson—and wisely chose Jefferson's River as their route. They began to search in earnest for the Shoshoni. They needed guides and horses desperately to cross the mountains before the autumn storms. Sacagawea recognized a landmark and assured them they would soon find her people. Lewis took three men and pressed on ahead of the Corps to look for them.

After five days they came upon "three female savages" to whom they offered gifts: "some beads a few mockerson awls some pewter looking-glasses and a little paint." This assured their welcome two miles on when sixty mounted warriors came thundering up. The men politely embraced Lewis; "we wer all carresed and besmeared with their grease and paint till I was heartily tired of the national hug."

When Clark and the rest joined them, an astonishing coincidence was revealed. The captains called for Sacagawea to interpret for them and the chief Cameahwait: " . . . she came into the tent, sat down, and was beginning to interpret, when in the person of Cameahwait she recognised her brother: She instantly jummped up, and ran and embraced him, throwing over him her blanket and weeping profusely: The chief was himself moved, though not in the same degree." The Corps had stumbled onto the very band from which she had been kidnapped.

From the Shoshoni, the captains bought horses and borrowed a guide, an old man who said he had learned the way long ago. Cameahwait explained how Nez Percé hunting parties suffered in crossing the fearsome mountains now called the Bitterroots, but Lewis thought "if the Indians could pass these mountains with their women and Children, . . . we could also. . . ."

They would also suffer. The trail was dreadful, and soon there was snow. Even today, when packers have trails beaten into the mountains, a ride through this country reinforces your respect for the Corps. I found the going treacherous on an October visit. Your horse's head, nodding in front of you, dips as you descend a precipitous slope, across slippery boulders, through mud, across fallen, rotting timber. The clatter of his hoofs on the rocks, his blowing and whinnying, the rush of a stream, the

"Encamped opposit a Small Island," wrote Clark of this site on the Lochsa River during the arduous traverse of the Bitterroots. Horses often slipped and fell on a trail slick with mud or snow. Food ran out: "here we were compelled to kill a Colt for our men & Selves to eat . . . we named the South fork Colt killed Creek"— a name that survives in local memory.

chatter of a gray squirrel, can take you back years, and you can almost see the men in buckskin tiring among the same obstacles.

According to Clark, they passed "up & Down Steep hills, where Several horses fell, Some turned over, and others Sliped down . . . one horse Crippeled & 2 gave out. with the greatest dificuelty risque &c. we made five miles & Encamped." One falling horse smashed Clark's portable field desk. Fallen timber blocked the trail in a mad jumble: " . . . high ruged mountains in every direction as far as I could see," he wrote. Water gave out and the men had to melt snow. Food ran low: soup and bear's oil. This was worse than towing pirogues up the Missouri, worse than the portage around Great Falls. This was about as bad as it could get. "I have been wet and as cold in every part as I ever was in my life," wrote Clark; "indeed I was at one time fearfull my feet would freeze in the thin Mockirsons which I wore."

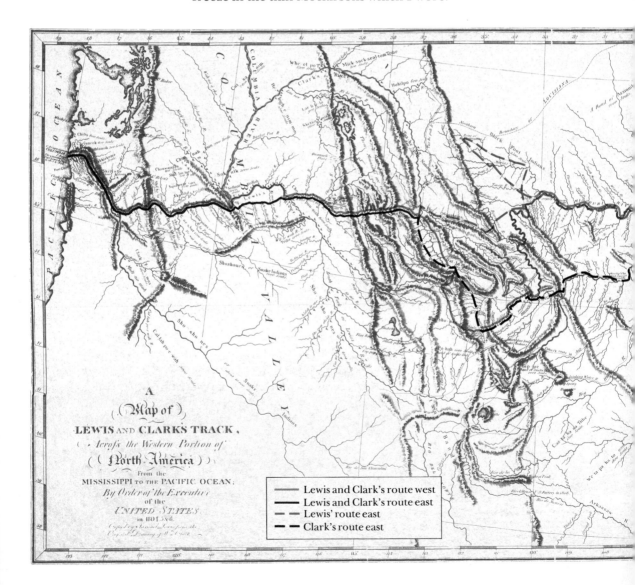

Rivers and mountains previously unknown sprawl across the West on the first official map of the country opened by Lewis and Clark. Clark—an astute and skilled geographer—drew

Finally, on a cold but sunny September 18, Clark looked out from a summit and saw an "emence Plain and *leavel* Countrey." The ordeal of the Rockies was behind them.

They were befriended by a village of Nez Percés who provided food—flour made from camas root, and salmon. The flour gave nearly everyone dysentery, but the salmon meant rivers that led to the ocean. The Corpsmen made pinewood dugouts to resume travel by water—this time *with* the current: down the Clearwater to the Snake, the Snake to the Columbia.

Now a new hazard faced them: rapids on a scale that not even Cruzatte, their best boatman, had ever seen. Anxious to make good time, they ran rapids they should have portaged.

At one reach of the Columbia, now famous as The Dalles, the great river passed between steep cliffs just 45 yards apart and portaging was impossible "with our Strength." Clark wrote, "I

Overleaf: Red men and white exchange greetings on the lower Columbia River. As Lewis and Clark approached the Pacific, they found much evidence of the coastal Indians' contact with whites. This Chinook party included "two Indians verry finely Dressed & with hats."

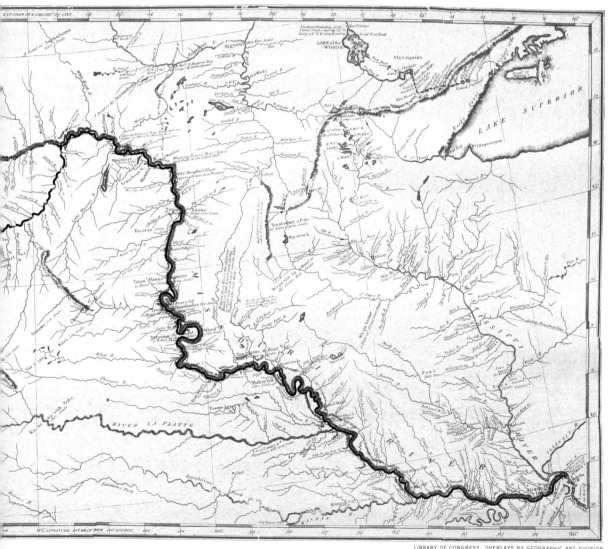

LIBRARY OF CONGRESS, OVERLAYS BY GEOGRAPHIC ART DIVISION

the original in 1810. Colored lines indicate the explorers' routes. On the return journey, the party split up temporarily, Lewis to explore the Marias River and Clark the Yellowstone.

deturmined to pass through this place notwithstanding the horrid appearance of this agitated gut swelling, boiling & whorling in every direction." Astounded Indians watched from the cliffs as the entire party entered the rapids—and ran them safely.

With mounting excitement the captains began to recognize signs of nearing the ocean. On October 21 they saw an Indian wearing a "Salors Jacket," and two days later "Great numbers of *Sea Otters*." Within a week Clark saw "a British musket, a cutlash and Several brass Tea kittles." A month after that they met a Chinook woman with *J. Bowman* tatooed on her arm.

A novel torment caught them on the lower Columbia. Clark noted glumly: "The Seas roled and tossed the Canoes in such a manner this evening that Several of our party were Sea sick."

Surging waves battered the canoes as they neared the river's mouth. The men were about as miserable as they had been in the Bitterroots. They inched along down the river, clinging to the north shore, as rain and storms drenched them. Sheer cliffs descended almost to high-tide line, making it nearly impossible to find campsites. The monstrous waters often held them up for days, huddled in the rain barely above the reach of the tide, hungry and cold, living on roots and dried fish they managed to obtain from the Indians.

But the day had come—November 7—when Clark jotted in his field notes: "*Ocian in view*! O! the joy." In fact he couldn't quite see the ocean yet; the huge estuary had fooled him. But except for exploring around the river's mouth and finding a place to spend the winter, the trip was over. They had done it, crossed the continent safely; and while they were probably too tired and hungry and cold to feel much joy, their sense of accomplishment and relief must have been profound.

On November 26 they paddled across the enormous river to the south shore. They began building a stockade, named Fort Clatsop for a local tribe of Indians, for their second winter in the wilderness. Lewis noted evidence that ships visiting the area were either English or American: "the Indians inform us that they speak the same language with ourselves, and give us proofs . . . by repeating many words of English, as musquit, powder, shot, nife, file, dammed rascal, sun of a bitch &c."

The explorers moved into their fort, snug and warm beneath the dripping spruce trees, on Christmas Eve, 1805; and the next day, feeling a little sorry for themselves, dined on "pore Elk, so much Spoiled that we eate it thro' mear necessity, Some Spoiled pounded fish and a fiew roots."

White-winged and common scoters battle gale-force winds over 16-foot waves in the mouth of the Columbia. Surf in the estuary rivals that of the ocean, but Lewis and Clark often saw Indians in specialized seagoing canoes blithely navigating such waters—"the highest waves," said Clark, "I ever Saw a Small vestles ride." Here the westward trip ended. The Corps spent the winter of 1805-1806 near present-day Astoria, Oregon.

Visiting Fort Clatsop, I found that the moist dark earth smells of springtime even in January, and pale-green lichens cover tree trunks like a living version of frost. This is the rainy season in Oregon, and I could see why the explorers found winter long and dismal. It rained every day but 12 in the three months they were there; fleas brought in by the Indians nearly drove them crazy; and the Indians themselves proved thievish and bothersome. The captains sent small parties of men to the sea to make salt, and one day a large group—including Sacagawea, who thought it "verry hard" that she had come all this way and still not seen the ocean—made the two-day trek to the beach to view the carcass of a whale that had washed ashore.

With spring, the Corps of Discovery turned for home. It was an eventful and exciting trip, but anticlimactic in a way. They had already accomplished what they had set out to do. They had laid to rest once and for all the myth of a water route across the continent, and had given the young United States a stronger claim to the land around the mouth of the Columbia River.

Word of their successful return spread across the country, and Americans everywhere were proud and excited. Citizens wrote tributes to the captains, comparing them to Columbus—not such a far-fetched comparison, really—and the captains responded with grace and humility, attributing their success not to their skill or courage but to Providence.

But even before they got home, the effect of their exploration was beginning. In August they had met two trappers traveling upriver. One of the men, John Colter, asked permission to leave the Corps and join the trappers. Permission was granted, and so began a trickle that would turn in time to a flood, as more and more trappers and adventurers headed west. But because of the expedition of Lewis and Clark, Colter was the first—when he turned back toward those astonishing mountains—to know where he was going.

Turning his back on home and comfort, John Colter waves good-bye to the men of the Corps of Discovery. He had spent two years with them, making the trip to the Pacific, but as they neared Mandan country again he opted for a life of adventure in the mountains; with Lewis's and Clark's permission, he joined two trappers heading west. He would later win renown as the discoverer of the geysers of Yellowstone National Park.

Teton sunset flares on the skyline of Jackson Hole, Wyoming, long a favorite among the many

6   A Reckless Breed:

western valleys explored and admired by the mountain men—audacious trappers of the fur trade.

the Mountain Men

By MICHAEL W. ROBBINS

"We shall die here, we shall never get out of these mountains." The young fur trapper, named White, had ample reason for despair. Like his companion, Osborne Russell, he lay arrow-shot and bleeding in the night near Yellowstone Lake. Late on an August afternoon in 1839, they had been hunting elk when a Blackfoot war party swept down screaming.

"...an arrow struck White on the right hip joint I hastily told him to pull it out and [as] I spoke another arrow struck me in the same place but they did not retard our progress. At length another arrow striking thro. my right leg above the knee benumbed the flesh so that I fell with my breast accross a log." Russell added: "I was very faint from the loss of blood and we set down among the logs determined to ... die like men."

Instead, they lived like the mountain men they were. Their Blackfoot attackers lost them in a thicket of fallen trees. The ambush was over, but the survival test had just begun. Without horses, without supplies, White and Russell and a Canadian trapper were many days' ride from help. Alone, they rose to the occasion. Their triumph is a classic of mountain man lore.

"I had bathed my wounds in Salt water and made a salve of Beavers Oil and Castoreum which I applied to them This had eased the pain and drawn out the swelling in a great measure. The next morning I felt very stiff and sore but we were obliged to travel or starve...."

They shot waterfowl and deer as they crept westward, Russell on improvised crutches. He commented: "I could limp along half as fast as a man could walk but when my foot touched against the logs or brush the pain in my leg was very severe."

Limping twenty to thirty miles a day, they reached Jackson Lake, then climbed and crossed the Tetons in the snow, and forded the Snake River. Game grew scarce and they traveled in hunger. Russell's leg began cramping so severely he could manage only yards between rests. Ten miles from Fort Hall (Idaho) they met a half-breed with horses who took them in. After resting for ten days, Russell returned to trapping.

Mountain men were tough.

They were the true pioneers of the West. Not the wagon-borne sodbusters, the cowboys, Mormons, or Forty-Niners. They were the explorers who put the region on maps for all the "pioneers" who followed. It was mountain men—beaver trappers—who found South Pass, who strode the Great Divide, who pushed across the deserts into old California, who brought back the eyewitness visions of geysers and boiling springs, of the Sierra and Yosemite.

They pushed west after beaver pelts and from 1820 to 1840 carved out a legendary way of life.

Jedediah Smith was forever marked by a grizzly that sprang upon him in a thicket west of the Black Hills. It grasped him by the head and broke several of his ribs before it was killed. Smith was all but scalped by its teeth. He was laid bare from left eye to right ear. One eyebrow was gone and one ear nearly severed. Smith, calmly directing his own repair, had one of his men use a needle to stitch the ear on. Within days he was back on his horse and heading west.

Crossing the Nevada desert in 1834, a brigade of trappers under Captain Joseph Walker, "apprehensive of perishing for water" themselves, watched with horror as their dogs died of thirst with "piteous and lamentable" howls. Lost, the brigade reached such an extremity of thirst that, a survivor reported, "whenever one of our cattle or horses would die the men would immediately catch the blood and greedily swallow it down." Their horses finally smelled the fresh stream that saved them.

These two, Jed Smith and Joe Walker, were leaders among the hundreds of mountain men. It was a legendary company of hunters, trappers, and explorers that included Kit Carson, Jim Bridger, Etienne Provost, Joe Meek, Thomas Fitzpatrick, David Jackson, and Andrew Henry. Their names became the vocabulary of our maps of the West. They went up the streams and over the next mountains because in two centuries "westering" had become American instinct. They went for the adventure. And the fur. Once there, they stayed on through the decline of the beaver trade because they came to love the bittersweet life in the mountain wilderness.

Smith and Walker were more than trappers and "captains." They became explorers, literally pathfinders: Smith was first to walk overland to California. He was in the group that found South Pass in 1824 and made it known as the key to Oregon. He was first to mark a direct route across the Great Basin, to traverse the Sierra Nevada, and to walk the length of California into Oregon. Joe Walker crossed the Nevada desert tracing what would become the California emigrant trail. He made it over the Sierra barrier into northern California. On the way in he discovered Yosemite and on the way out he traced the Walker Pass–Owens Valley route. Walker went on to lead wagon trains, to survey routes for the transcontinental railroad, to guide one of Frémont's surveys, to go prospecting even in his sixties.

These were men in whom the impulse to wander was strong. Walker's clerk, Zenas Leonard, wrote: "to explore unknown regions was his chief delight."

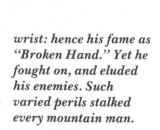

To escape a Blackfoot attack in 1836, Thomas Fitzpatrick lunges down a riverside bluff—into an ordeal. In his scrambling, desperate haste, he shot and shattered his own left wrist: hence his fame as "Broken Hand." Yet he fought on, and eluded his enemies. Such varied perils stalked every mountain man.

It's still a delight, even in our age of satellite mapping. It persists in contemporary mountain men like Lance Grabowski and Jon Judd, who live the style of the originals. In anyone who itches to see the country—even in me. I wanted to see the land where these explorers walked, to make their "unknown regions" known to me. Not to live off the land but to hike and look. Not to go after beaver . . . but maybe after trout.

The beaver trade spawned explorers. It was lucrative—and intensely competitive. The strategy of the Hudson's Bay Company was simply to trap out Rocky Mountain streams before the Americans got there. Whole watersheds were emptied of the prized creatures. So each year enterprising men probed a different zone of the mountains, seeking untrapped streams.

Under the American system developed by William Ashley and Andrew Henry, the trappers stayed in the mountains working the beaver country spring and fall, holing up in winter, and being resupplied each summer at a riotous rendezvous. The most ambitious men and prosperous companies underwrote year-long exploration trips, broader sweeps to the west. Smith led two, in 1826 and 1827. Walker led one in 1833.

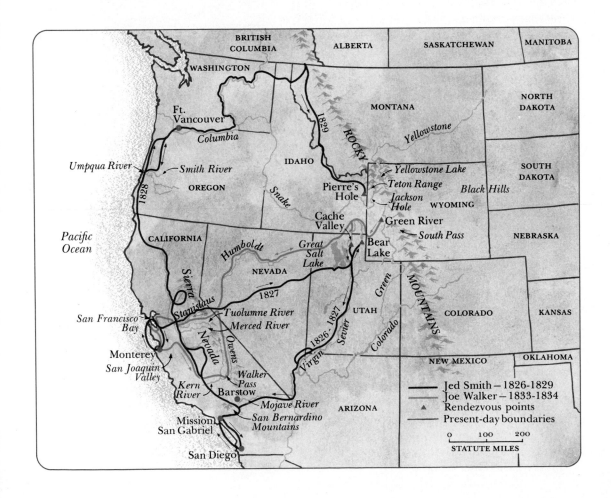

Smith served a brief apprenticeship. He signed on with Ashley's brigade in 1822 and after one year had proven himself a leader, a "captain." At the rendezvous of 1826 he became a partner in an enterprising fur company, the celebrated Smith, Jackson, and Sublette. The partners divided their tasks for the coming year. Smith was chosen to strike into the unknown territory to the south and west of Salt Lake. He was serious, methodical; he kept a journal: "I with thirteen men went to the SW for the purpose of hunting B*er* [beaver] but not finding them plenty enough to justify me in Stopping I pushed on through a Country of Starvation."

His troop left the Cache Valley rendezvous in mid-August. They rode southward for a week, then followed the Sevier—which Smith called Ashley's River—upstream. Naming features as they went along, they rode west along Clear Creek, crossed a divide, and headed toward the Beaver River and a dry inhospitable land of sterile hills. By the time they reached the red rock walls along the Virgin River, they had finished their 700 pounds of buffalo meat. They were "sometimes 2 or 3 day without half a meal" and Smith wrote: "I had lost so many horses that we were all on foot . . . worn out with fatigue & hardships & emaciated with hunger."

Ten days down the Virgin River, they came to the Colorado and followed it into the country of the Mohave Indians. They found no beaver.

White men were no novelty even here. Among the Mohave were Indian deserters from California missions. One of Smith's men spoke Spanish and, Smith wrote, "I found that it was not far to some of the Missions of California & I detirmined (as this was the only resort) to go to that place as soon as my men & horses should be able to travel."

They followed the Mojave River and, as was usual in "exploring" inhabited country, a trail. Sixteen days on the ancient Indian trade route took them to the San Bernardino Mountains. They had trekked across genuine desert: In the Mojave the sun's heat reflects upward not from billowing dunes but from eternally gray flats where low clumps of sage merge with distance to form a dark stubble.

Joining Lance Grabowski, a rawhide modern-day mountain man, I had occasion to try their trail. Few of the big facts of the desert have changed since 1826: The sun is implacable. Water is scarce, precious. The clustered sage is fragrant but scarcely high enough to shade one's ankles. The air is so clear that vision seems intensified into hawk-like resolution. The mountains seem close, but an hour of hiking brings them no closer.

Lance was concluding his 1,400-mile ride, a commemorative

Jedediah Smith (1799-1831) and bearded Joseph R. Walker (1798-1876) blazed southern and northern routes to the Pacific. In 1826, Smith led the first

Americans overland into California— Mexico's then. He died in a Comanche ambush. Walker, Tennessee-born, struggled across the Nevada deserts and Sierra Nevada snows; he lived out his days in California.

rerun of Smith's journey from northern Utah to San Bernardino. Smith's type of travel, he said, is finished. People have been everywhere and left their tracks and trash. Ironically, Grabowski noted, "you can't follow Jedediah Smith's trails" and capture his experience; because Smith succeeded, the paths he found have become railroads and highways.

Walking in a shallow Mojave valley outside of Barstow, I began to grasp western distances and to understand the price of a mistake. On foot a man makes so little impact on these spaces and at such a cost in resources. If he errs and misses the next water, he could step, step, step to the last flicker of his energy and, as he fell, see no change in the indifferent desert. A wrong turn elsewhere might mean a loss of time. Here it could mean a loss of life.

Smith's party followed their guides and the Mojave River—which Smith named the "Inconstant" for its tendency to disappear and flow underground—to its source. They walked up out of the desert's shimmer and into the brown hills. They began to see trees and grass . . . an abundance of fresh water! They saw cattle then, and horses tended by Indians.

They had walked into California.

On that day in late November when Jedediah and his weary men trooped into the Mission San Gabriel, it was at the peak of its development. To these men out of the desert, the contrast could not have been more striking, between hot aridity and lush cultivation: "thousands of acres of Rich and fertile land." Farms were scattered over the Mission's far-flung land, with "upwards 30,000 head of cattle, and Horses sheep Hogs &c in proportion." The Mission itself was practically a village with a church, workshops, and amenities: ". . . they have large vine yards, Apple and peach orchards . . . some orrange Trees and . . . they distill whiskey and grind there own grain. . . ."

Smith's troop came as a surprise, but they were welcomed: ". . . introduced to the 2 Priests over a glass of good old whisky—and found them to be Joval friendly Gentlemen."

An American century has transformed the vineyards and pastures to Los Angeles suburbs, but the Mission church is scarcely changed: sanctuary, altar, pulpit, baptismal font are the same. And the Mission remains a home of hospitality. When I stopped on a warm weekend, the Claretian Fathers were holding their annual Labor Day carnival and, under the sun and bright banners, the gardens rang with music and laughter.

Frustration in granite to westering explorers, this maze of Sierra Nevada valleys offers no easy passage. Joe Walker's dogged brigade groped its way up from the desert in 1833, only to find what Walker's clerk Zenas Leonard described as "everlasting snows on the summit" and "no practicable place for crossing."

Away from the celebration, I sat in a quiet office with Father Leo Mattecheck. Between whiffs at his pipe, he told me that the Mission has "only the documentary evidence" of Smith's visit—with the possible exception of a small trap, reportedly found years ago on Mission property. But, he remarked, visitors come each year, following Smith's trail.

That it leads northward foreshadows events to come. With his band of armed men, Smith had explored his way onto Mexican soil. The Governor—"much of a Gentleman but very Suspicious," said Smith—probably saw them as harbingers of trouble with the United States. He excused their unauthorized intrusion on condition that they leave immediately, by their entry route. But they were still eager for a good trove of beaver pelts, so when they set out in January 1827 they swung north. They continued northward until May—the snow was too deep for a crossing of the Sierra.

Finally Smith decided to leave most of his party in California. He would go to rendezvous with Silas Gobel and Robert Evans, seven horses and two mules. They started on May 20.

Despite a snow pack eight feet deep, they traversed the high country in eight days.

A month of walking in the Nevada desert cost them all but one horse and one mule. Reduced by hunger, fatigue, and thirst, they found trudging in soft sand "almost insurportable." They resorted to digging holes in the sand and lying in them to cool off. They walked all night. They very nearly didn't make it: "at 10 O Clock Robert Evans laid down in the plain under the shade of a small cedar, being able to proceed no further. We could do no good by remaining to die with him and we were not able to help him along, but we left him with feelings only known to those who have been in the same situation. . . ." Just three miles farther, Smith and Gobel found water. Smith walked back to Evans with a small kettle of water that saved his life.

On the afternoon of July 3, Smith walked into the rendezvous near Bear Lake: "My arrival caused a considerable bustle."

Rendezvous!

"Beaver the currency of the mountain, was plenty that year, and goods were high accordingly," said an eyewitness. "A thousand dollars a day was not too much for some of the most reckless to spend on their squaws, horses, alcohol and themselves."

Each midsummer, supply caravans from Missouri met up with hundreds of trappers and Indians from all over the Rockies. By agreement they converged on a campsite with game, grazing, water, and elbow-room. They would stay for weeks, trading a year's harvest of pelts for a year's supply of necessities: coffee, sugar, tobacco, "whiskey." Blankets, knives, traps, guns and ammunition. It was a fair, an impromptu town, a Saturnalian trade show. A celebration of having survived.

"In the beginning of their spree many feats of horsemanship and personal strength were exhibited," reported Joe Meek, a colorful character even by mountain man standards. "But the horse-racing, fine riding, wrestling, and all the manlier sports, soon degenerated into the baser exhibitions of a 'crazy drunk' condition. . . ." These men were "chock full of brag and fight," and they played rough. They fornicated, gambled, lied, settled "affairs of honor," and just plain fought.

New Englander Nathaniel Wyeth pronounced them "a great majority of Scoundrels." Others took a more relaxed view. Sir William Stewart, a Scottish officer, concluded "that 1833 was the last good year, for with 1834 came the spoilers—the idlers, the missionaries, the hard seekers after money."

I fished the Green River, then called the Siskadee, near the sites of six rendezvous. I know why they came back here repeatedly—it looks like the inspiration for the anthem's "fruited plain." The river is shallow and cool; the meadow grasses and willow thickets along the banks would be good forage for horses and mules. Some white-faced steers watched me solemnly as I pushed through the brush, seeking good casting into the riffling water. Waiting for the elusive cutthroat trout, I thought about the long caravans heading this way from South Pass, about the nightmare attack by rabid wolves in '33. Somewhere along this looping stream Kit Carson won his duel

MAURICE HORNOCKER

"They no sooner see you than they will make at you with open mouth"—a warning by Zenas Leonard against the grizzlies of the

Rockies. Among the mountain men who tangled with these unpredictable predators: Jed Smith and "Broken Hand" Fitzpatrick.

with the bully Shunar, and Dr. Marcus Whitman dug an old Blackfoot arrowhead from the back of stalwart Jim Bridger.

I wondered whether Jedediah Smith liked the rendezvous. He was without recorded vices and maybe without a sense of humor. Joe Walker loved them, the brawling and dealing. But in 1827 Smith tarried at rendezvous only ten days—to gather men and horses for his second overland walk to California.

This time he would avoid the "Country of Starvation," taking a "More circuitous route" along the rivers: the Provo, the Beaver, the Virgin and the Santa Clara to the Colorado. He and his 18 men reached the Mohave villages in mid-August.

He had no way of knowing their "hearts were bad." Only later did he learn that Mexican authorities had warned them

A Trapper's Gear

Tools of the fur trade enabled mountain men to survive and go after pelts—as in this 1837 painting by eyewitness artist Alfred Jacob Miller. A hollowed cherry branch (right) held castoreum, a glandular secretion prized as a beaver lure. Iron traps like this 1830's example caught the animals; trappers used steel butcher knives to dress hides. Smaller implements, carried in a leather "possibles bag," helped to keep men warm, clothed, and armed: an awl for stitching leather; a striking flint and a handle-like steel striker for starting fires; a bullet mold for .50-caliber lead balls—and

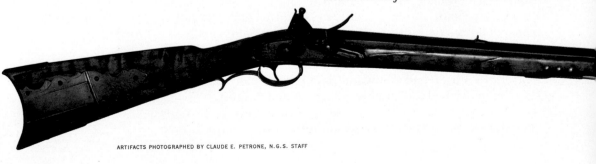

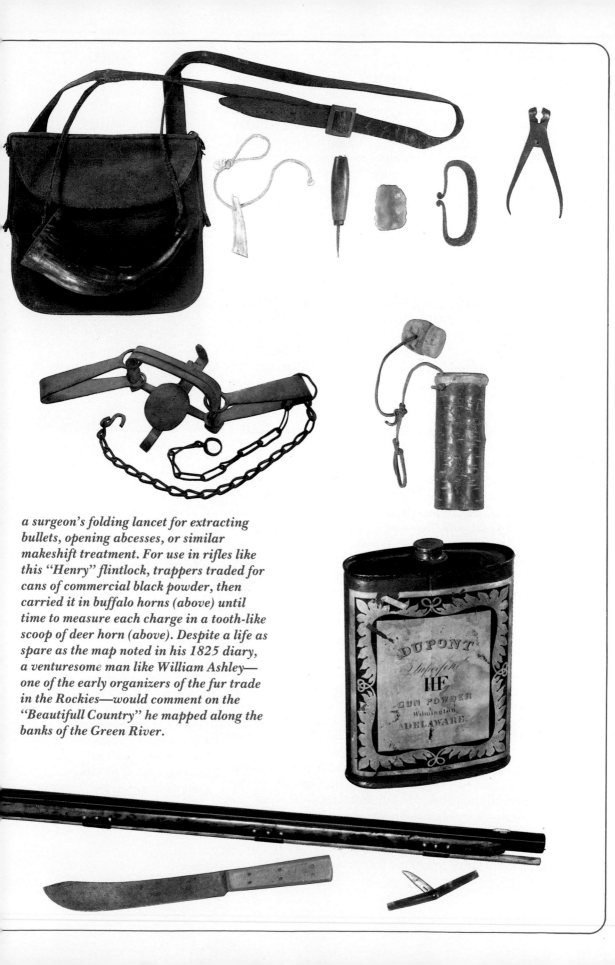

a surgeon's folding lancet for extracting bullets, opening abcesses, or similar makeshift treatment. For use in rifles like this "Henry" flintlock, trappers traded for cans of commercial black powder, then carried it in buffalo horns (above) until time to measure each charge in a tooth-like scoop of deer horn (above). Despite a life as spare as the map noted in his 1825 diary, a venturesome man like William Ashley— one of the early organizers of the fur trade in the Rockies—would comment on the "Beautifull Country" he mapped along the banks of the Green River.

DUPONT
Superfine
HF
GUN POWDER
Wilmington
DELAWARE

not to let any more Americans enter California. The Mohave were capable dissemblers. For three days, as they built rafts to cross the Colorado, Smith's men suspected nothing. When Jedediah and eight men got out to a sandbar, the Indians struck—they slaughtered the ten left on the bank. Within minutes the survivors were cornered in a riverbank thicket, facing hundreds.

"With our knives we lopped down the small trees . . . to clear a place in which to stand, while the fallen poles formed a slight breast work. We then fastened our Butcher knives with cords to the end of light poles so as to form a tolerable lance, and thus poorly prepared we waited. . . . It was a fearful time. Eight men with but 5 guns were awaiting . . . the charge of four or five hundred indians whose hands were yet stained with the blood of their companions.

"Some of the men asked if I thought we would be able to defend ourselves. I told them I thought we would. But that was not my opinion."

Against all the odds, Smith's tactics worked. "Seeing a few indians who ventured out . . . within long shot I directed two good marksmen to fire they did so and two indians fell and another was wounded." That courage and marksmanship stampeded the Mohave.

Now there was the desert to face, without horses or supplies. Incredibly, the nine Americans did reach California in August—much to the annoyance of the Governor.

After some weeks of awkward interviews with the authorities, they hurried north, to find the waiting group of trappers on the Stanislaus River. The united party gathered supplies, bought horses at $10 to be sold at rendezvous for $50, and started northward on December 30, 1827.

This was genuine exploring; there were no maps. They found beaver sign, and did as much trapping as a score of men could manage with only 47 traps among them and a herd of 300 horses and mules to tend to. Tangled mountainous terrain seemed every mile to show some new obstacle—until rain and fog closed in. Through a difficult winter they earned every northward mile.

The journals of Smith and his clerk Harrison Rogers are daily summaries of hardship. "The rain that commenced the day before continued without intermission for 24 hours." ". . . so exceedingly rocky and rough that I was four hours in moving one mile." "In a bad pass. . . . two of my horses were pushed from a precipice into the river and drowned."

Rogers' account ends abruptly, as did his life. By early summer of 1828 the party had reached Oregon, and on July 12 they camped on the Umpqua River. Smith and Richard Leland and John Turner went off scouting the river. Rogers was in charge of the camp two days later when some two hundred Kalawatset Indians arrived. Judging them friendly enough, he let them into camp—and suddenly they fell on the trappers, killing all but one.

Seeking untrapped streams, young Jed Smith leads his men southwest from Cache Valley in 1826 through an unknown "Country of Starvation." With Indian aid, Smith's men—who included a slave listed only as John—became the first Americans to complete an overland crossing to California. Sixteen blazing days of walking took them across the Mojave Desert to Mission San Gabriel.

Turner, Leland, and Smith, with only the clothes on their backs, walked or staggered 150 miles through the forest to the Hudson's Bay Company outpost on the Columbia River. There, at Fort Vancouver, they met the other survivor, Arthur Black. The Company's factor John McLoughlin treated them generously; it was a party he organized that punished the attackers and salvaged many of the beaver pelts, some of the horses—and the journals.

Reading those matter-of-fact journal accounts—and seeing these beautiful sites—I had to wonder at this reckless breed of men. They were frontier-bred, most of them, but there's little in their background to show why they chose that life.

Jedediah Strong Smith was born in the final year of the 18th century in the thinly settled frontier. From his birthplace at Bainbridge, New York, his family made its way to the Western Reserve (now in Ohio). They were Yankee westering farmers with deep religious convictions. Little else is known. By the time Jed left home in 1821 he was probably a capable hunter.

In the February 13, 1822, issue of the *Missouri Gazette &*

"Close to
the
Original"

Taking the measure of Jed Smith's epic trek, modern mountain men Lance Grabowski and Jon Judd ride out of a Utah forest in 1977. To get "the feel and experience" of that exploit, Lance and Jon planned a two-month journey "as close to the original route" as possible. It proved a severe test of their handmade gear, their horses, and themselves; one month on the trail lamed Jon's horses, ending his share in the adventure. "Original mountain men didn't have to do what they did either," observed Lance. "But they were incredibly self-reliant, tough, and independent." Feeling that independence—and some trail weariness—Jon (left) and Lance rest at a campfire. At Bear Lake, vicinity for the trappers' rendezvous in 1827 and 1828, they enjoy the quiet rewards of time alone in "Beautifull Country."

Public Advertiser, Gen. William H. Ashley placed his famous advertisement for "Enterprising Young Men" to venture up the Missouri. That appeal all but opened the West.

Jedediah signed up. He was soon seen as a man to be counted on. He was not especially colorful. But he loved the wild. LeRoy Hafen, the dean of the historians of the American fur trade, summarized his admiration for Jedediah as a "good man, with a Bible in one hand and a gun in the other. And he wrote beautifully. Beautiful letters!"

To those who knew Smith—and to those who've come to know his accomplishments—he was the stuff of legends, the mountain man's mountain man.

It is another who shows how their era ended.

Joseph Reddeford Walker was born on December 13, 1798, on a Tennessee homestead. Growing up a frontier youth, he "rode, shot, trapped, hunted, plowed and harvested...." The family moved to western Missouri, a raw land in 1818. The boys became farmers and traders. Joe went west for the first time in 1820, to trade in New Mexico.

He was 34, and tough, when he went to the Rockies. He had met Capt. Benjamin Louis Eulalie de Bonneville and they had formed an alliance. Bonneville, an Army officer on detached service, was eager to explore—and follow the fur trade.

They started from Missouri with 20 wagons full of goods in May 1832, and within a year they concluded that the way to turn a profit was to go to California. Bonneville made Walker a "captain," put him in charge of a "brigade" of fifty trappers, and sent him to explore the way west and to find beaver. Walker's brigade rode west from the Green River rendezvous on July 24, 1833. Indians warned them that only desert lay ahead.

"Exploring" is a flexible term. Often there was someone around who knew the neighborhood. Walker's clerk Zenas Leonard noted that they met Indians who advised them to follow their paths "to find water without much trouble."

The friars of the Domínguez-Escalante expedition had had much the same experience; and the mythical "Buenaventura River," shown on Miera's map as emptying into the Pacific, was something Walker was supposed to look for. He thought it would be the Humboldt of today. In the desert of the Great Basin, there were still Indians scratching out a living as in the past. Some followed the brigade, and stole beaver traps. Some of the party wanted vengeance. They didn't dare let the captain know; but when they encountered a few Indians, they shot to kill.

Keeping a fractious Kenotay to a walk in the parched Mojave, Lance Grabowski completes a 1,400-mile ride. Along the way he met with hardships like those of 150 years before: searing heat and soaking rain, insects and dust. He got lost; he suffered minor injuries and deep exhaustion—but he pushed on to California.

The
Golden Land

Young señor *and* señorita *turn gracefully in a traditional courtship dance—painted with dash and sentimentality in the 1850's. Around them swirl all the elements of the life that captivated Smith's and Walker's trailworn trappers: music, wine, showy horsemanship, lovely women. While many ranch families and friars at the missions showed warm hospitality, the Mexican civil authorities looked with suspicion on aliens who*

CHARLES C. NAHL, "THE FANDANGO"; E. B. CROCKER ART GALLERY, SACRAMENTO

came armed. They detained Jed Smith, questioned him, and asked him to leave. Their fears proved well-founded: Within three decades of his arrival, California had become an American state. Today at Mission San Gabriel, a statue honors friars and converts; a cross marks holy ground where six thousand Indians lie buried. The missions brought not only their faith but also a stern rule, an alien life.

Walker learned of it too late. The damage was done. The brigade found itself at bay facing a great war party, perhaps as many as 900 men. Even the veteran trappers grew edgy. At last, "greatly excited," Walker ordered a charge. Thirty-two of his men attacked a group of eighty or more Indians, killed 39, and dispatched the enemy wounded with their own arrows. Thereafter the Indians showed no aggression.

From "Battle Lakes"—the site in the Humboldt sink—the brigade could see the snow-topped Sierra Nevada rising like a mile-high wall to the west. Hunters were sent to find game, scouts to seek a route into the mountains. No game; no pass. In October a scout finally discovered a promising "Indian path." The Walker party followed it.

Thus began what has been called "the worst passage in our westering." It consumed more than three weeks. Game was nonexistent, snow already very deep, cold at night bitter. The men ate the horses that broke down, then killed their own mounts. They grew mutinous, wanted to turn back. Walker refused. They stuck it out, and kept climbing west.

Finally, on high ground, they could scan a vast distance back east across the Basin. But ahead . . . as far as they could see there was only a bleak jumble of granite ridges and peaks and snow-choked hollows.

Preceding pages: Rendezvous! Festival, trading session, and a spree that one historian calls "maleness gone berserk." Each summer from the mid-1820's till 1840, the mountain men would meet one another, traders from St. Louis, and Indians at a selected valley. They swapped pelts and supplies and "skull varnish" liquor, bets and brags and lies, squaws and horses.

This was exploring: "We were at a complete stand. No one was acquainted with the country, nor no person knew how wide the summit of this mountain was. We had traveled for five days since we arrived at what we supposed to be the summit—were now still surrounded with snow and rugged peaks—the vigor of every man almost exhausted. . . ."

They followed the sharp ridge lines between chasms, between the watersheds of the Merced and Tuolumne Rivers. Probably they were the first white men to gaze the awesome mile down into Yosemite. Finally, near the end of October, they came to the western brink of high country. They found game. And a descent so steep they had to let the horses down one at a time, secured with ropes. They inched down to the San Joaquin Valley, and by mid-November they were staring at the Pacific.

They had made it. But they had not found much beaver, and they had not found the "Buenaventura" passage they hoped for.

At Monterey a new Governor welcomed them. The men relaxed, repaired their gear, admired the horsemanship and the dances of the Californians, and traded for supplies. Some—like millions of easterners to come—decided to stay.

Walker, itching to move on, shrewdly looked for a new route back, a southerly route. He engaged Indian guides, and a four-day march along the South Fork of the Kern River led to the

In a deadly melee called the Umpqua Massacre, Jed Smith's men fight for their lives on July 14, 1828. Only one got away. Oregon Indians known as Kalawatset had entered the camp as if to trade—and attacked by surprise. What had altered their earlier friendship remains both obscure and hotly argued. Smith, off scouting that morning, escaped and obtained Canadian help.

"His Chief Delight"

At "the extreme end of the great west," a Yosemite sunset transforms valley clouds to a surf of radiance and reveals a powerful lure of the mountain man's life: the beauty of a spectacular land. After a visit to civilization, Jed Smith expressed his elation: "...so long absent...and so much perplexed and harrassed by the folly of men in power I returned again to the woods...with a feeling

somewhat like that of a prisoner escaped from his dungeon and his chains." One of Joe Walker's men wrote of him: "to explore unknown regions was his chief delight." Walker, among the first Americans ever to gaze on these mountains and "incredibly large" sequoias, found them profoundly moving. More than forty years later, he ordered inscribed on his gravestone the words "Camped at Yosemite."

mile-high pass that now bears Walker's name. A final rocky ascent, and he and his men looked out on the Mojave Desert.

Once a route for emigrants and freight wagons, Walker Pass today is a junction for a twisty two-lane road and the Pacific Crest Trail. I hiked up the trail for an hour, then climbed directly to the peak. I wanted to see where Walker had been and where he had gone. Around the Kern River is a jumble of peaks and draws, a confusion. To the east the desert is flat, rose and gray. The steady wind carries a dry, hot scent of pine.

With one Indian battle—which Walker regretted, but won— the brigade returned eastward. They reached Bear River on July 3, 1834. A week later Bonneville arrived with his supplies and high expectations. He was disappointed. Walker's men had had a great adventure; they had discovered useful routes across the desert and over the mountains. But the pelts they brought back didn't even cover their wages.

Bonneville and Walker had a better year after that but never made the big profits in furs. His journey marked Walker as a reliable guide to the west beyond the Rockies. Like many trappers he stayed on after the beaver trade died about 1840. They used their dearly won knowledge of the wilderness to guide caravans of settlers—and to usher in a new age. Walker guided that celebrated "pathfinder" John Charles Frémont for a while in 1844, and led him to California in 1845. Walker continued to explore remote corners of the wilderness until he was in his sixties. Restless to the end, he died and was buried in California.

Jedediah Smith never reached old age. He packed all his exploring, all his miles and close calls, into a single decade that closed when he was just 32. Seeking water for a trading party bound for New Mexico, he was ambushed and killed by Comanches. What he learned about the west passed on, by word of mouth, to later maps and explorers.

Now the wilderness has been explored and named. People live here. Among the trappers' most important finds was that here a special good life is possible. I caught its flavor from a guide, Dave Hansen, who came west to Jackson Hole from Iowa, "took a look and decided to stay." He took me out on the Snake River, and I finally caught some trout. I found that he knew all about Jedediah Smith and Jim Bridger, Joe Walker and "Broken Hand" Fitzpatrick. They were his heroes and he had already spent fifteen years in the Rockies—as long as they. He had become a versatile outdoorsman. He knew why the mountain men had come and stayed. And what they found.

On a workaday route turned playground, young horses rollick in Kern Valley, California. Joe Walker discovered this wide valley; it climbs to the Sierra Nevada pass that still bears his name. In his time, Walker Pass brought freight wagons from the Mojave to the Central Valley. Relatives of his still reside in the area.

Sandhill cranes, migrating north in April, fly at dawn above the Platte River in

7   John Charles Frémont:

Nebraska, an area first scientifically mapped by John Charles Frémont in 1842.

Maps for the West By THOMAS O'NEILL

Gone were the sounds of animals and men, and darkness hung over the prairie like a great tent. No campfires flickered; only the high grass moved. John Charles Frémont knew he was lost.

Hours earlier, the excitable young surveyor had joined in his first buffalo hunt. The scene was the far-flung prairie near Fort Pierre, and the year was 1839. As a new member of the Army's Corps of Topographical Engineers, Frémont had come west to help map the land between the Missouri and Mississippi Rivers. That summer afternoon the camp hunters had sighted buffalo on the uplands, and, eager to get along in his prairie education, Frémont rushed to the chase.

As the horsemen rode at breakneck speed, he remembered, "the only things visible to me in our flying course were the buffalo and the dust. . . . I made repeated ineffectual attempts to steady myself for a shot at a cow . . . and each time barely escaped a fall."

When the dust had finally cleared, Frémont discovered himself to be alone, out of sight, lost. Nightfall found him tired and solemn. At midnight, as he trudged along a buffalo path, he saw a rocket splash in the sky. It was a signal from his comrades, a fiery sign of rescue. Confident that he could find his way by daylight, he fell asleep on a prairie bed.

Upon his return to camp, he showed no embarrassment; instead, he seemed proud that the wilderness had presented him with an adventure to remember. "I had made an experience and it had ended well," the 26-year-old surveyor concluded. The next night he wrote happily: "This was the Fourth of July. I doubt if any boy in the country found more joy in his fireworks than I did in my midnight rocket. . . . Water and wood to-night were abundant, and with plenty in camp and buffalo all around we celebrated our independence of the outside world."

For Frémont, who would become one of America's great explorers, getting lost served as a rite of passage. The incident crystalized his impulsiveness, his love of adventure, and his ability to find significance, even romance, in almost everything he experienced. These traits, added to the scientific skills he was acquiring, would guide his future exploits as a pathseeker and help create his fame. He would continue getting lost throughout his career, and more often than not his wanderings would serve him well.

He led three notable government expeditions between the years 1842 and 1846, during which time he was responsible for

Sweetwater River tumbles through Devil's Gate, in central Wyoming. While mapping the Oregon Trail in 1842, Frémont rode through this cleft

PAINTING BY JOSEPH GOODHUE CHANDLER;
THE OAKLAND MUSEUM HISTORY DEPARTMENT

and remarked on the contrast of the verdant river valley with rocky gorge and sandy plain. His own life offered contrasts even more startling. By turns he gained and lost fame, fortune, and political favor. A portrait from about 1850 shows him in his late thirties.

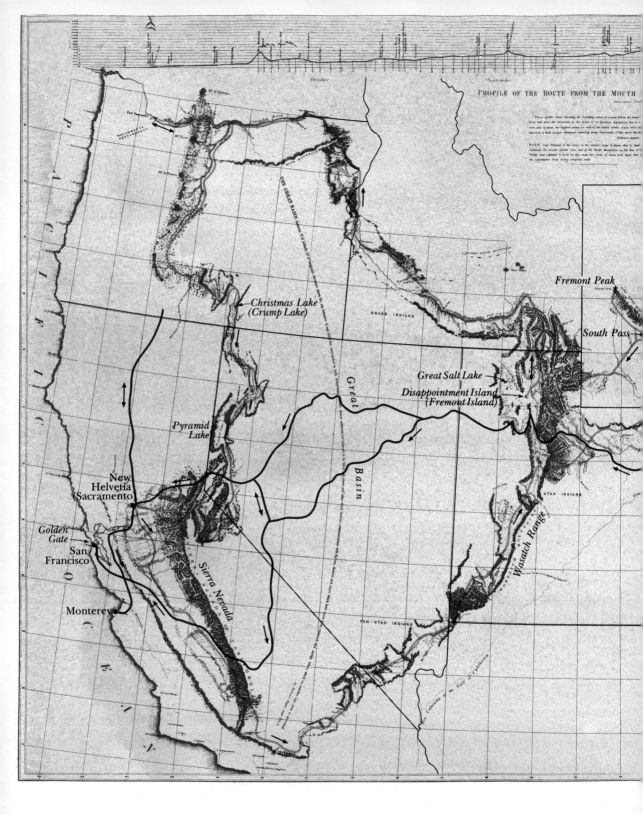

October

September

Fremont Peak

South Pass

Christmas Lake
(Crump Lake)

SNAKE INDIANS

Great Salt Lake

Disappointment Island
(Fremont Island)

Great

Pyramid
Lake

UTAH INDIANS

Basin

New
Helvetia
(Sacramento)

Wasatch Range

Golden
Gate

San
Francisco

Sierra Nevada

Monterey

PAH-UTAH INDIANS

Landmark of cartography, Frémont's map from his second
expedition shows only the areas he actually traveled and
leaves the remainder blank. Thus it does not copy errors of
fact and fancy found in earlier maps. Instead, he based his
work on astronomical observations using accurate instruments. To achieve precision, Frémont on occasion worked
for hours in deep snow with telescope and chronometer in

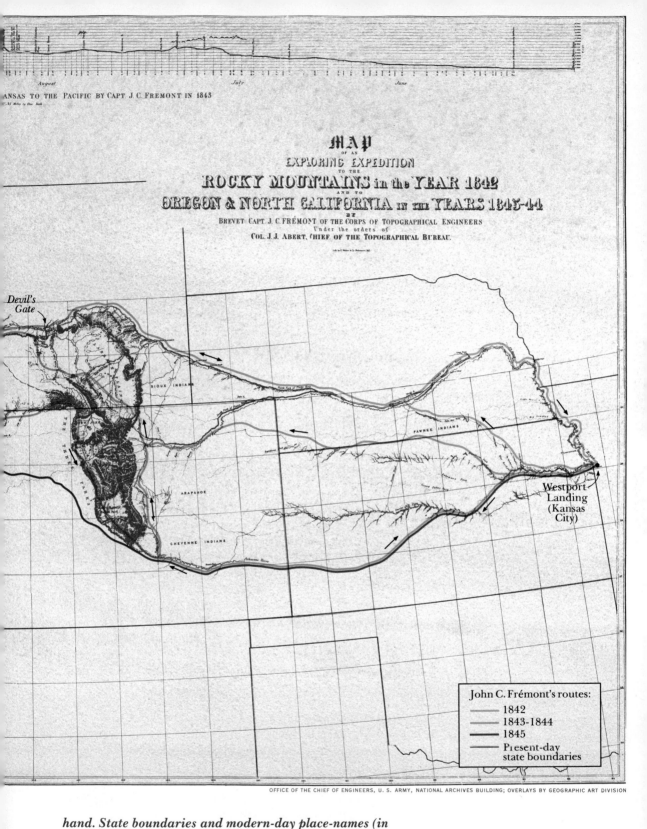

*hand. State boundaries and modern-day place-names (in
parentheses) added to his map dramatize the extent of his
three major expeditions, their routes superimposed in
colors. Besides his major achievement—providing reliable
maps and appealing accounts of the Oregon Trail—his gift
for the vivid phrase lives on in the name he gave to the
entrance to San Francisco Bay: the Golden Gate.*

mapping and describing more of the West than any person before him. He traveled the length of the Oregon Trail to map it for the emigrants; he withstood hunger and thirst so he could determine the nature of the Great Basin; and he struggled across the Sierra in the thick of winter, striking a path into California.

For a month I traveled Frémont's many paths, tracing more than 4,000 miles by car, foot, and horseback. I watched the rivers, plains, deserts, mountains, and forests go by—the features of the West that Frémont made believable to an eager public.

Dr. Donald Jackson is a scholar of the American West who talks about the early trailblazers with as much enthusiasm as sandlotters give to past World Series. At his home in Colorado Springs, he explained to me how Frémont marked a dividing line between amateur and professional exploring: "Sure, Jed Smith, Jim Bridger, and others had seen all the places before. But their business was catching beaver and muskrat, and any information brought back was incidental to their fur packs. Frémont's role was to refine what was already known. He went down all those trails with professional instruments. That was his real job."

Just as influential as his mapping was his reporting: stirring tales of lush valleys and towering mountains in Oregon and California. These reports captured the imagination of the country. As much as any one person in the 1840's, Frémont convinced Americans they ought to take their wagons west.

As if destined to wander, Frémont was born in 1813 to a pair of unwed lovers drifting across the South. The father, a Frenchman called Charles Frémon, and the mother, Anne Whiting Pryor, wife to a prominent Revolutionary War veteran, had scandalized Richmond society when they ran off together in 1811. When John Charles was born in Savannah, they had established a pattern of wandering from town to town, the father giving lessons in French and dancing, the mother tending boardinghouses.

At 16, with his father dead and his mother poorer than ever, John Charles entered the College of Charleston, where he showed a flair for mathematics. His ardor for romance proved greater, though. Persistent courting of a dark-eyed Creole girl led to frequent absences from class; three months before graduation, the young man was expelled.

Restless and undisciplined, Frémont—who added a "t" to his name, and took pride in the French accent—was saved from floundering by his friendship with Joel R. Poinsett, a well-

JEFF FOOTT

"We were soon involved in the most ragged precipices," wrote Frémont of his party's attempt to scale the Wind River Range (opposite). "We clambered on, always expecting, with every ridge that we crossed, to reach the foot of the peaks, and always disappointed...." That same day, the cold and hungry explorers thought they heard a bleat like that of a young goat. But upon eager investigation, the men found a different— and far less palatable— source for the sound: a pika, like the one above munching a bluebell. The outcome: "We had nothing to eat to-night."

Frémont conquers "the highest Peak of the Rocky Mountains"
in an engraving that captures his quicksilver flamboyance
while erring in every detail: his clothing, the flag and staff,
and the fact that dozens of peaks in the Rockies rise higher.

connected diplomat who had returned to Charleston after serving as his country's first minister to Mexico. In 1836, Poinsett arranged for his protégé to take a surveyor's job in the southern Appalachians, then one in Cherokee territory in backcountry Georgia. From these projects Frémont concluded that his fortunes would be made "among the Indians and in waste places."

As Secretary of War in 1838, Poinsett arranged for Frémont to accompany the French scientist Joseph Nicollet on surveys of the upper Missouri and Mississippi River country. These trips were his Yale College and his Harvard, Frémont recalled in later life. From the voyageurs he picked up frontier lore—how to manage camp, hunt and skin buffalo, escape prairie fires, deal with Indians. From Nicollet he learned how to take astronomical and barometric readings, sketch field maps, and collect botanical and geological specimens. Professional skills were now aligned with a passion for the outdoors.

The most auspicious meeting of Frémont's young career took place inside an office in Washington, D. C. Recently commissioned a second lieutenant for the Topographical Corps, Frémont was working on Nicollet's map when Senator Thomas Hart Benton paid a call. Benton, a blustery but high-minded politician from Missouri and one of the most powerful men on Capitol Hill, was known as the spokesman for westward expansion. True to form, the Senator unfurled his vision. It is the nation's special calling to people the new lands of the West, Benton exhorted—the message later known as Manifest Destiny. In these high-flung words Frémont espied a meaningful role for himself. It would be to "travel over a part of the world which still remains the New," he wrote, "opening up of unknown lands; the making unknown countries known; and the study without books."

Frémont soon became a regular visitor at the Benton household, not only to hear the Senator with rapt attention but also to catch the eye of daughter Jessie. Lovely and vivacious, Jessie at 16 had already received two proposals of marriage. But she was most taken with this dashing young officer. Jessie and John fell deeply in love despite the iron opposition of Benton, who wanted a son-in-law of means. In October 1841 the couple secretly married. When Benton found out, he ordered Frémont from the house. Clutching her husband's arm, Jessie cried with Biblical passion the ancient pledge "whither thou goest, I will go. . . ." Finally Benton relented. With this dénouement, Frémont gained in Benton a great patron and in Jessie a steadfast wife and champion of his career.

A pragmatic man behind the posturing, Benton set about to put his son-in-law to work. Congress appropriated $30,000 for a reconnaissance of the Oregon Trail as far as South Pass in the

Frémont's most ardent supporter, his talented wife Jessie, passionately defended him against all detractors—including President Lincoln. Through her father, Senator Thomas Hart Benton of Missouri, Frémont won leadership of his first expedition. Jessie helped write her husband's widely popular reports, and her own books and articles sustained the family in the 1870's during years of extreme poverty.

Rocky Mountains. Nicollet's health was failing; the expansionists saw Frémont as a suitable replacement. According to the Army, the aim of the expedition was strictly scientific: to map the route and fix the position of the pass. Benton imagined more dramatic results: to advertise the promise of Western lands and to assure emigrants of government support and protection.

The expedition set out in June 1842 from a spot now part of Kansas City. As the men rode north and west across the plains, averaging 20 miles a day, Frémont had every reason to feel exultant. At 29 he had his first command, the weather was beautiful, buffalo were plentiful, and adventure seemed imminent. Only two emigrant wagon trains had preceded him on the route.

The prairie casts a spell of motion, and I succumbed, racing toward the horizon. My path to the Rockies, like Frémont's, followed a line of rivers—the Vermillion, the Big and Little Blue, the Republican, the Platte, the Sweetwater. Unfortunately, most of his campsites are buried under concrete or lost in cattle pastures. Yet the huge, cloud-strewn sky, the curling rivers, and the long uneventful distances all evoke that earlier journey.

Frémont's party included one other man of science. This was Charles Preuss, 39, a red-faced, fastidious German topographer. Most of the 28 were mountain men and voyageurs, glad to continue their outdoor living on government wages now that the fur trade had dwindled.

Most notable of the ex-trappers was Kit Carson, hired as a guide for $100 a month. At 32 this sandy-haired frontiersman had already roamed most of the West. Short in size, he was long in deed, famous among the mountain men as deadly in both buffalo hunting and Indian fighting. He could neither read nor write, but spoke French and Spanish as well as Indian dialects. To the rash and passionate Frémont, the cool-headed and efficient Carson served as a perfect counterweight.

It was early August when the troop reached South Pass, the portal to the Far West. For some reason expecting an alpine gorge, Frémont registered clear disappointment when he sighted this wide saddle at the Continental Divide in what is now central Wyoming. He compared the ascent to the climb of Capitol Hill, and left without taking measurements. According to orders, the expedition was now to about-face and return east. For the first and not the last time, Frémont ignored orders and followed the rule of his passions. He headed his men northwest to the Wind River Range, no doubt confident that its magnificent peaks would supply adventure—and good copy for his report.

From my vantage point at South Pass, the Wind River Range again appeared irresistible. I took to the hoof and rode into the country with Rob Hellyer as wrangler, George and Paula Hunker as guides.

"Grab onto the mane and lean forward so that horse can get up the slope easier," shouted Rob, a lanky cowboy. I obeyed, and the buckskin mare clambered up the rocks like an ungainly mountain goat. As we rode over meadows and forded streams, I felt taken with what Frémont called the "gladness of living." At 9,000 feet, the yellowing aspen leaves quivered in the breeze and the sun forced our shirtsleeves up. Two thousand feet later, our horses were high-stepping through three feet of snow and our fingers curled in our gloves. Only the calendar said summer.

As we pushed farther, the landscape showed gray rock and white snow. The few sounds we heard were the lonely whinny of a hunter's horse and the reedy call of a pika, or mountain rabbit. I remembered what George, a thoughtful, tobacco-spitting outfitter, had said: "I guess you're an explorer if you are just driven to see what you haven't seen before."

After two days of riding we reached the foot of Fremont Peak, a monolith lifting 13,730 feet, draped with snow as it was the day Frémont and his men scrambled along the ridge. We dismounted, and started our ascent. Soon my sea-level lungs felt tight as a fist. Halfway up, we began to sink to our thighs in snow; each step demanded a decision. After three hours of exhaustion, we reached the top. I was seeing what I had never seen before: a breathtaking vista of glaciers, frozen lakes, and soaring peaks.

"Take this." Paula handed me a grape drink, and with time for a few gasps of hurrahs, we hurried down in a driving storm.

Frémont tarried on the summit to plant a flag "where never flag waved before," and share a round of brandy with his men. He would declare in his report that he had scaled the highest peak in the Rockies. In fact, dozens are higher. Moreover, a climbing party in 1951 matched his descriptions with its own observations and concluded that the mountain he conquered is not the one that bears his name but a nearby peak named for Woodrow Wilson.

Never one to shun a chance for adventure, Frémont on the return trip decided to take six men in a rubber boat and shoot the rapids of the Platte. Crowing Canadian boat songs, the crew steered through rapid after rapid. Then the boat hit a submerged rock and flipped. The foaming river took all his scientific journals. Luckily, duplicate records were contained in journals held by the main party.

Safely in Washington, Frémont and Preuss turned out a map based on 68 observations for latitude and longitude, and a table with more than 600 meteorological readings. Impressive as these were, they were almost overlooked in the gale of excitement stirred up by the accompanying 207-page report. Western chronicles up to then had either been accurate but dry, like the Lewis and Clark effort, or flavorful but touched with hearsay, such as the books by Washington Irving. With Frémont's report, literary flair and scientific authority joined forces.

At first John Charles penned the words himself. But he soon complained that the indoor exertion afflicted him with nosebleeds and headaches. He and Jessie, a talented writer, would become a team—in later years he dictated and she polished.

With each page Frémont put the West in sharper focus. He described the terrain, the weather, soil and water, vegetation and wildlife. He advised where forts should be built and where the good campsites could be found. He acclaimed the fertility of the Great Plains. This doused for good the notion of the Great American Desert, a theory publicized by Maj. Stephen H. Long after an expedition in 1819 and 1820. Frémont had become on this trip the first government surveyor to take along a daguerreotype camera, but he did better with word pictures. The Wind River Range appeared as "a gigantic disorder of enormous masses, and a savage sublimity of naked rock, in wonderful contrast with innumerable green spots of a rich floral beauty, shut up in their stern recesses."

Frémont was the trumpeter of the West, and the public wanted to hear. Congress ordered extra copies of the report, and newspapers printed generous excerpts. "Nicollet's pupil turned exploration into a grand national spectacle," Dr. Jackson told me.

"He combined the scientific bent of his mentor with the PR instinct of his father-in-law, and that was an unbeatable combination when the wagon trains were ready to head west."

Meanwhile Frémont was preparing for another Benton-inspired expedition. Orders called for Frémont to return to South Pass and then push on into the Oregon country. In May 1843 the officer and 39 men commenced their westward journey. From their 14 months in the field emerged a map that was a milestone in American cartography. Drawn by Preuss, it supplied the public with a first reliable look at the skeleton of western geography. The vast vague tract between the Wasatch Range and the Sierra Nevada for the first time bore the inscription "Great Basin," reflecting Frémont's important conclusion that here "the rivers and lakes . . . have no communication with the sea." The river drainage of California began to take on accurate shape, and it was Frémont who would give the entrance of San Francisco Bay the title "Golden Gate."

By confining the map to areas seen firsthand, Frémont and Preuss established an important precedent, and their work bore the signature of science.

To gather readings, Frémont unveiled the disciplined side of his character and spent hours—sometimes waist deep in snow—with telescope, sextant, and pocket chronometer. He rarely discussed his instruments in his reports. Yet in a time when

Christmas 1843: In the Oregon country, the second expedition celebrates with a salute from a howitzer brought along against orders and soon abandoned in deep snow. The holiday luxuries: sugar, coffee, and brandy—"one of the most useful articles a traveller can carry," Frémont remarked.

satellites, lasers, and computers dominate mapping, it is the mention of the old techniques that nostalgic mapmakers perceive as almost the stuff of romantic literature.

"Before World War I, the field topographer was king, a member of the aristocracy," remembered Robert Foley, a cartographer with the U. S. Geological Survey in Denver. "Now your field surveys are supplementing the aerial photographs. The map goes through twenty people and what you do as an individual is largely lost." I showed him a copy of a Frémont map. He slowly nodded his head: "You could look at a map and know whose it was. It was like a work of art."

David Danculovich has never seen his name on a map. Yet as a field surveyor for the Geological Survey—a successor to the Topographical Corps—he can see himself as an heir of the Frémont legacy. "One of Frémont's basic problems was figuring where on the face of the earth he was," David was saying as he steered a pickup truck down a gravel road. "He didn't have today's network of triangulation stations and benchmarks." Our position on the face of the earth that day was sagebrush desert north of Douglas, Wyoming; and David, his assistant Sabrina Furman, and I were heading out for a day of measuring. The 54-square-mile area known as the Bill Quadrangle was being remapped, and David was spending his summer gathering "ground truth." This involves such details as determining the elevation of a windmill that will become a key point of reference.

Looking from my window, I watched a band of pronghorns sprint across the scrub. Lightning began to flash over a ridge to the north. The country appeared so uniform, so desolate, that I wondered aloud why a new map was needed. "When the last was made around 1955," David replied, "there were no oil wells, no uranium mines, no coal mines. Now on this sheet we'll have all three. There's a heck of a lot of new stuff out there." Thus the energy explorers become the latest emigrants.

Walking to a benchmark, David checked a map. His glasses came out and he squinted hard. Some 25 years of staring at maps for the government have taken a toll on his eyes. I asked if he minded the changes in field methods. "You know, I fit a whole lot better in a helicopter than in a saddle," he admitted. "I can rent a helicopter that will drop me off near a peak, do what I have to do, and I'm back in the office for a coffee break." What he does envy about Frémont's days in the West is the absence of people. Gaining access to private property poses David's biggest headache.

Frémont's path westward in 1843 generally followed the deepening wheel ruts of the Oregon Trail. It was the year of the

Wavelets soften evening shadows of the great rock that prompted Frémont to name this body of water Pyramid Lake, in today's northwestern Nevada. "For a long time," he wrote of that January afternoon in 1844, "we sat enjoying the view...."

so-called Great Migration, when a thousand people took the emigration highway. On occasion, the expedition would veer off to test a new route, or explore a river's course, or, as in late summer, to lay eyes on the little-known Great Salt Lake. With characteristic flush, Frémont called it "a magnificent object . . . to travellers so long shut up among mountain ranges, a sudden view over the expanse of silent waters had in it something sublime."

Two days later the leader and five of his men navigated a leaky rubber boat to a large island, now named for Frémont. Reduced to such food as stewed skunk, he was looking forward to getting game. Finding none, he called it Disappointment. As consolation, his men boiled down 14 pints of salt—a luxurious supply—and he took readings that resulted in the first undistorted map of the lake. His published description of the surrounding Bear River basin enticed the Mormons to settle here.

Some of his voyageurs thought that a great whirlpool linked the lake by underground channels with the Pacific. "The whirlpool—we've just passed it," Utah State Park ranger Stephen Olsen was saying with a cocky grin. Just then, with a terrific jolt, our boat rammed to a stop on a sandbar. Stephen insisted he would free it himself, so I waded half a mile through the clear water to Frémont's desert island. I wanted to see a cross Kit Carson had carved on a rock while waiting for Frémont to finish his stargazing. Unfortunately, the island was four and a half square miles, the cross at the far end, the time late afternoon.

Impulsively, I started on. I watched with delight as a herd of wild ponies dashed off at the sight of me, and I enjoyed the fragrance of sage. But as the sun dropped, my spirits did likewise. I was a prisoner of schedules. Moreover, the island was private property, and I had no permission to spend the night. As I waded back to the boat, I yelled, "I rename you—Disappointment Island!"

On November 8, 1843, Frémont reached Fort Vancouver on the Columbia River, final stop on the Oregon Trail. Here he saw a stream of arriving emigrants, now less than a day's travel south to the "land of promise"—the verdant Willamette Valley. Nearby he heard "with pleasure" the sound of a sawmill at work.

At the end of the month, he gathered his rested men and proceded south along the Sierra. According to orders, he was to take his men home. But in the middle of January, at a spot south of Pyramid Lake, he announced that he wanted to cross the mountains to California. At a glance, and even a stare, the notion seemed mad. It transgressed orders; provisions were low and horses exhausted; the central crest of the Sierra loomed ahead, covered with deepening winter snow. Yet Frémont's bold impulsiveness seemed to take hold of him again. More to the point, he knew a restless public was clamoring for news of California.

The way proved torturous. Horses and mules slipped off icy canyon walls. Indian guide after Indian guide deserted the white men in fright. The hungry killed and ate their starving horses and dogs. Frostbite and snowblindness began to appear.

On February 6, Frémont and a scouting party climbed on snowshoes to the top of a broad promontory south of Lake Tahoe: "Far below us, dimmed by the distance, was a large snowless valley, bounded on the western side, at the distance of about a hundred miles, by a low range of mountains, which Carson recognized with delight as the mountains bordering the coast." The Sacramento Valley had been sighted at last.

It was a tattered, hollow-cheeked band that reached the valley in early March. "The starvation and fatigue they had endured rendered them truly deplorable objects," reported Captain John Augustus Sutter, the Swiss settler whose fort served as their point of collapse. Of 104 mules and horses, only 33 remained. One man had wandered off in a crazed fit of cold and hunger, but had been rescued. Once again Frémont had been lucky. By Sierra standards the winter had been mild.

Still, Sutter's fertile tract of 50,000 acres—today the site of the city of Sacramento—vividly illustrated the promise of California, and Frémont would publicize it in his second report.

The homeward trip proved largely uneventful. (It produced Frémont's great geographical blunder, a statement that freshwater Utah Lake was an arm of the Great Salt.) When he returned to civilization, he had completed the most spectacular tour of the West since the journey of Lewis and Clark.

Back home, Frémont and his wife collaborated on another spirited report. The response was overwhelming. By the spring of 1845, when the "Pathfinder" set off on his third expedition, he had bloomed into a national hero.

The politics of expansion had been heating up. War was

"Good God! Look there!" exclaims Kit Carson as an Indian crone appears before the campfire north of Walker Pass in 1845, during the third expedition. She "had thought it a camp of her people," who had abandoned her, Frémont noted. Given food, she bolted into the darkness.

Snow-mantled conifers cast lengthening shadows on a December afternoon in the Sierra Nevada.

Frémont crossed this range nearby in early 1844, en route to California's Sacramento Valley.

brewing with Mexico over the annexation of Texas; the U. S. and Britain were sparring over title to 500,000 square miles of the Oregon country, which in 1846 would be divided at the 49th parallel; and James K. Polk, the new President, showed strong interest in California, which the Mexicans held but weakly.

On the way west Frémont duly explored the course of the Arkansas River, spent a fortnight surveying the Great Salt Lake, and struck a new trail across the broken plateau of the Great Basin. Once in California, however, he dropped the scientific guise. Without knowing whether the Mexican War had begun or not, he organized his 60 men into an armed force and proceeded to play a prominent role in the American takeover of California.

His exploits ended in a court-martial. He recognized the authority of Commodore Robert Stockton, USN, who claimed overall command, and did not obey Gen. S. W. Kearny, whom Polk belatedly backed up. The vindictive general charged Frémont with mutiny. Not since the Aaron Burr sensation in 1807 had a trial received so much national attention. In January 1848 the tribunal found Frémont guilty. Polk braved Benton's fury to uphold the verdict, but canceled the punishment. Insulted and indignant, Frémont resigned from the Army.

If his career had ended with his last explorations, his place in history would be more comfortable than it is today. The court-martial did not sully his name, and at age 35 he was a celebrated explorer. Yet his career had peaked. Misled by his own fame and tripped up by the ways of the world outside the wilderness, he strayed from his skills as scientist and pathmarker. In the last half of his life he tried business, politics, and war. Failure seemed to attend almost every move he made.

His greatest business entanglement centered around a huge estate in the Sierra foothills, bought for $3,000. Gold was discovered on his property; he became a multimillionaire. Bad business deals and conniving associates siphoned off much of the fortune before he sold out in the early 1860's.

Because of his radical antislavery views—learned from Poinsett and Benton—and his national glamour, the newly-formed Republican Party chose him to run for President in 1856. "Free soil, free men, and Frémont!" Unfortunately, he showed no aptitude for politics. Victory went to James Buchanan.

Frémont proved just as ineffectual as a military leader in the Civil War. President Lincoln in 1861 appointed him to run the Department of the West, with headquarters in St. Louis. Inept at handling large quantities of men and money, and undermined by sniping from political enemies, the beleaguered major-general was relieved of command after just three months.

None of his railroad ventures worked out. His postwar efforts to promote a line between Norfolk and San Diego left him penniless. In his later years, only Jessie's prolific authorship of articles and books kept them out of poverty. On July 13, 1890—

Preceding pages: Breaking trail, an advance party struggles through the Sierra Nevada. Across the valley, the other men and pack animals follow. To prevent snowblindness, the explorers swathed their faces with black silk. This crossing cost Frémont 71 horses and mules—starved, slipped into canyons, killed for food. And one man went mad; his comrades saved him.

The Oregon Trail

Bound for a promised land, German immigrant families follow the Oregon Trail to the Rockies in 1863. The artist, German-born Albert Bierstadt, sought to convey what he saw as "the wildness and abandon of nature"; a companion admired the "bright and comely faces" of the people. All told, about half a million pioneers took this route. This tide of settlers changed the character of the West. Once known to few but the Native Americans who lived there and the adventurers who traded with them, it had become a realm of opportunity. The Homestead Acts sped the pace of expansion, and federal surveying teams supplanted the trappers, mountain men, and explorers who had fired the imaginations of countless Americans with reports of daring exploits and natural wonders in the blank spots on the map.

when railroads were carrying passengers across the continent and hundreds of new communities had sprung up across the West—John Charles Frémont, almost forgotten, died in a Manhattan boardinghouse.

Seen from the historical armchair, Frémont was a man of large successes, large failures. He was brash, talented, and forever restless; he was hardy, resilient, and imbued with a touch of the knight, a touch of the clown; he was a man after all who seemed to embody the character of his country as it awkwardly and powerfully began to emerge as a great nation. His maps and reports served as powerful catalysts for the settling of the West. What was once a vast, mysterious territory between the Mississippi River and the Pacific Ocean became comprehensible and compelling because of his work. Hundreds of thousands of pioneers would eventually cross the country on the Oregon Trail, many of them carrying the Frémont maps on their laps and his descriptions in their heads.

With Frémont's work, a great saga of American exploring came to an end. By the middle of the 19th century, the major features of the country were known, and it would be left to a new generation of government surveyors, men like John Wesley Powell and Ferdinand Hayden, to fill in the last white spaces.

On a bright, windy autumn day, I pulled into the town of Cokeville, Wyoming, only a few miles from the Idaho border. It is near the spot in the Bear River Valley where Frémont looked upon the inspiring scene of a string of emigrant camps, the white covers of the wagons dotting the edge of the woods for several miles. Tumbleweeds tagged along as I walked toward a cafe where five or six people were hunched over coffee. Between bites on a sandwich, I spread out a copy of one of Frémont's maps, and before long all the customers in the tiny restaurant had either clustered around my table or spun around on their bar stools to pepper me with talk. "Hey, Frémont camped right by my farm," tooted one fellow with a sun-cracked face. "You can see wagon-train tracks cutting across a corner of my father's land," chipped in a woman at the counter. Out spun their tales of mountain men, emigrants, founders of the town, all the stories told with the familiarity of gossip about high school chums.

I felt a bit giddy when the cafe door finally slammed behind me and I returned to the street. I felt close to Frémont, having met those who were fulfilling the explorer's wish that the valleys and the plains that he had admired would one day be peopled. Settling back behind the wheel, I found myself folding up the service-station maps, closing the road atlas. When I drove out of town, heading west, it was with Frémont's map spread at my side.

Sunlight glances off Fremont Peak in California, in the area where the lieutenant and his men first clashed with Mexican troops. Later conflicts overshadowed this bloodless face-off; but the acquisition of California opened the American West to those who followed the explorers, the first into the wilderness.

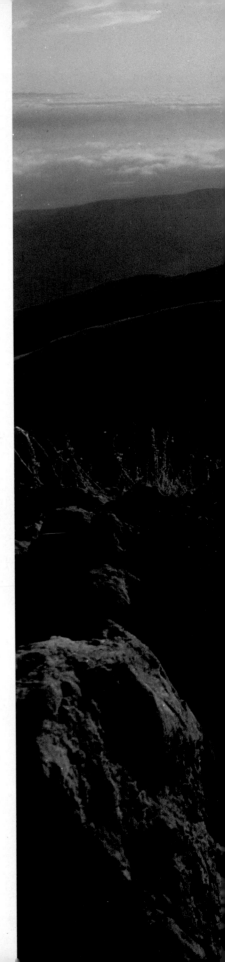

Contributors

RON FISHER has traveled explorer-style himself to write two Special Publications, hiking for *The Appalachian Trail* and canoeing for *Still Waters, White Waters.* Born and educated in Iowa, he joined the division's staff in 1966. He makes his home in Virginia.

LOWELL GEORGIA, now a resident of Arvada, Colorado, has carried out many assignments for the Society during his years as a free-lance photographer. As a picture editor on its staff, he was in charge of illustrations for the Special Publication *Discovering Man's Past in the Americas.*

A free-lance artist for more than twenty years, H. TOM HALL specializes in historical illustrations for books and magazines. He graduated from the Philadelphia College of Art, now lives and works in Chester Springs, Pennsylvania. In 1976 he illustrated *John Muir's Wild America* for Special Publications.

Brought up in Des Moines, JOHN HESS earned his B.A. and M.F.A. at the University of Iowa and served in the U. S. Air Force before making his career in publishing as a writer and editor. During 1976 and 1977 he worked for the United Nations in Nairobi, Kenya.

Born in Ohio, THOMAS O'NEILL grew up in Champaign, Illinois, and graduated from Beloit College in 1973. He worked as a reporter for the *Janesville Gazette*

and a free lance in Washington, D. C., before joining the GEOGRAPHIC staff as a writer in 1976.

City-bred and widely traveled, CYNTHIA RUSS RAMSAY has found "joy and satisfaction" in the wilderness regions of the West. Since joining the Society's staff in 1966, she has written for several Special Publications and served as managing editor of Books for Young Explorers (for children 4 through 8).

Free lance MICHAEL W. ROBBINS, brought up in Ohio, learned a taste for the wild and its skills from Indian guides in Wisconsin. He got his B.A. from Colgate, M.A. from Johns Hopkins, Ph.D. from George Washington University. Now an Easterner by residence, he "loves the West—the Rockies—the Pacific."

Investigative reporter RICHARD T. SALE lives in Washington, D. C., and has written numerous articles for the *Washington Post*. Growing up in Greenwich, Connecticut, he explored "woods next to the house." He earned a B.A. in history at Columbia, later lived with members of a South Chicago street gang to write his book *The Blackstone Rangers.*

EDWARD O. WELLES, JR., free-lance journalist turned newspaperman, grew up in Washington, D. C. He graduated in 1972 from the University of North Carolina at Chapel Hill, where he studied English and political science. In 1982 he moved to California and joined the staff of the *San Jose Mercury News.*

Index

Boldface indicates illustrations;
italic refers to picture legends

Acknowledgments

The Special Publications Division is grateful to all the individuals, agencies, and organizations named or quoted in this book for their generous cooperation. For chapter reviews: Thomas D. Clark, Joseph Ewan, Richard Glover, Fred R. Gowans, LeRoy R. Hafen, Charles E. Hanson, Jr., Victor G. Hopwood, Donald Jackson, W. Kaye Lamb, W. L. Rusho, and Marc Simmons. For special assistance: Stephen Dow Beckham, Theodore J. Brasser, Ian Church, C. Gregory Crampton, George Croteau, Theodore Dudley, Charles Fairbanks, Catherine S. Fowler, Dennis Gaarden, Stuart Holland, Bill Holm, Dale Lott, Fannie Mann, Grace McCarthy, David Northrup, Richard Ross, Albert H. Schroeder, Robert Scott, Shirlee Smith, Theodore Stern, Omer C. Stewart, Henry W. Toll, Jr., Ardis M. Walker, William C. Weneta, Barton Wright, and Henry Zenk. For extensive help throughout the preparation of the book: the Smithsonian Institution, particularly Henry W. Setzer, John C. Ewers, Betty T. Arens and the Costume Division; and the staffs of the American Philosophical Society, the Bartram Trail Conference, the Filson Club, the Hudson's Bay Company, the John Bartram Association, the Missouri Historical Society, the Museum of the Fur Trade, the National Archives, Old Fort William, the Oregon Historical Society, the Pacific Center for Western Studies, Parks Canada, the U. S. Forest Service, the U. S. Geological Survey, and the Utah State Historical Society.

Additional Reading

The reader may wish to consult the *National Geographic Index* for related articles, to see the Special Publication *In the Footsteps of Lewis and Clark,* by Gerald S. Snyder, and to refer to the following. **Primary sources:** *William Bartram, Botanical and Zoological Drawings,* Joseph Ewan, ed.; *The Travels of William Bartram,* Francis Harper, ed.; *The Field Notes of Captain William Clark, 1803-1805,* Ernest Staples Osgood, ed.; Fray Francisco Atanasio Domínguez, *The Missions of New Mexico, 1776,* Eleanor B. Adams and Fray Angelico Chavez, trans. and eds.; *The Domínguez-Escalante Journal,* Fray Angelico Chavez and Ted W. Warner, trans. and eds.; *The Expeditions of John Charles Frémont,* 4 vols., Donald Jackson and Mary Lee Spence, eds.; *Adventures of Zenas Leonard, Fur Trader,* John C. Ewers, ed.; *The Journals and Letters of Sir Alexander Mackenzie,* W. Kaye Lamb, ed.; *Original Journals of the Lewis and Clark Expedition,* 8 vols., Reuben Gold Thwaites, ed.; *Letters of the Lewis and Clark Expedition With Related Documents, 1783-1854,* Donald Jackson, ed.; *Charles Preuss, Exploring with Frémont,* Erwin G. and Elisabeth K. Gudde, trans. and eds.; *Osborne Russell, Journal of a Trapper,* Aubrey L. Haines, ed.; *The Southwest Expedition of Jedediah S. Smith,* George R. Brooks, ed.; *The Travels of Jedediah Smith,* Maurice S. Sullivan, ed.; *David Thompson, Travels in Western North America, 1784-1812,* Victor G. Hopwood, ed. **Secondary sources:** John Logan Allen, *Passage Through the Garden;* John Bakeless, *Daniel Boone;* Don Berry, *A Majority of Scoundrels;* Herbert E. Bolton, *Pageant in the Wilderness;* Thomas D. Clark, *A History of Kentucky;* Robert Glass Cleland, *This Reckless Breed of Men;* Gloria Griffen Cline, *Exploring the Great Basin;* W. P. Cumming et al., *The Exploration of North America 1630-1776;* Paul Russell Cutright, *Lewis and Clark: Pioneering Naturalists;* Harrison Clifford Dale, *The Ashley-Smith Explorations and the Discovery of a Central Route to the Pacific 1822-1829;* Frederick S. Dellenbaugh, *Frémont and '49;* Bernard DeVoto, *Across the Wide Missouri;* John C. Ewers, *Artists of the Old West;* Fred R. Gowans, *Rocky Mountain Rendezvous;* LeRoy R. Hafen, ed., *The Mountain Men,* 10 vols.; Harold A. Innis, *The Fur Trade in Canada;* Dale L. Morgan, *Jedediah Smith;* Allan Nevins, *Frémont.*

Library of Congress CIP Data
National Geographic Society,
Washington, D. C.
  Special Publications Division.
  Into the wilderness.

  Bibliography: p. 207
  Includes index.
  1. United States—Description and
travel—To 1783. 2. United States—Description and travel—1783-1848. 3. United States—History—1783-1865. 4. Canada—Description and travel—1763-1867. 5. Canada—History—1763-1867. 6. Explorers—United States—Biography. 7. Explorers—Canada—Biography. I. Title.
E163.N35   1978   973   77-93400
ISBN 0-87044-252-X

Composition for INTO THE WILDERNESS by National Geographic's Photographic Services, Carl M. Shrader, Director, Lawrence F. Ludwig, Assistant Director. Printed and bound by Holladay-Tyler Printing Corp., Rockville, Md. Color separations by Colorgraphics, Inc., Forestville, Md.; Graphic South, Charlotte, N.C.; National Bickford Graphics, Inc., Providence, R.I.; Progressive Color Corp., Rockville, Md.; The J. Wm. Reed Co., Alexandria, Va.; Sterling Regal, Inc., Carlstadt, N.J.